GUIDE FOR WORLDLY WOMEN

CONFIDENTLY PLAN THE PERFECT TRIP & TRAVEL INDEPENDENTLY

KAT HARRIS

D1739020

Copyright © 2023 by Kat Harris

All rights reserved.

No portion of this book may be reproduced in any form without written permission from the author except as permitted by U.S. copyright law.

This publication is designed to provide accurate and authoritative information in regard to the subject matter covered. It is sold with the understanding that neither the author nor the publisher is engaged in rendering legal, investment, accounting, or other professional services. While the publisher and author have used their best efforts in preparing this book, they make no representations or warranties with respect to the accuracy or completeness of the contents of this book and specifically disclaim any implied warranties of merchantability or fitness for a particular purpose. No warranty may be created or extended by sales representatives or written sales materials. The advice and strategies contained herein may not be suitable for your situation. You should consult with a professional when appropriate. Neither the publisher nor the author shall be liable for any loss of profit or any other commercial damages, including but not limited to special, incidental, consequential, personal, or other damages.

CONTENTS

INTRODUCTION

It was time to part ways. After spending ten days together in Thailand and Bali, three of my girlfriends stood on the curb and waved goodbye as I drove away in a taxi. They were heading home to California, and I was on my way to catch a one-way flight to Hanoi. Fresh out of college, I signed a one-year contract to teach second grade in Vietnam's capital city. I was teary-eyed, probably from a mix of nervous excitement and genuinely doubting if this move was too extreme, even for me. Friends and family back home had concerns. "You're going all alone? Aren't you scared?" The answer was yes. But I like that saying: *Feel the fear and do it anyway.*

Over the course of the past 15 years, I've swam with dolphins off the coast of New Zealand; driven on the left side of the road; slept in everything from backpacker hostels to 5-star resorts; seen temples beyond imaginable beauty in Cambodia; gone scuba diving in the Gulf of Thailand; figured out how to ride a motorbike; learned how to count to six in Vietnamese; handled pesos, riel, rupiah, baht, yen, dong, pounds, euros, and francs; sweated my butt off in the Balinese jungle; read about Buddhism; went on a yoga retreat in the Mai Châu mountains; cried when I missed home; drank beer for 50 cents a pint; trekked through rice terraces in Sapa; harvested apples in the English countryside; and participated in a summer solstice fire ceremony in Tulum.

All of these have been solo adventures.

It bums me out when I hear that women are too nervous or intimidated to travel alone. A healthy dose of caution is necessary, but an overwhelming fear that keeps you from living the life you imagine for yourself is a different story. Perhaps you're worried about personal safety or worry that you'll be lonely or isolated. Maybe you're concerned about navigating unfamiliar places or language barriers. Or maybe there is apprehension about cultural differences or discrimination and the belief that certain destinations may not be female-friendly or welcoming.

Listen, I get it. The media tends to highlight negativity, and if we hear one alarming story online, it scares us from venturing out alone. And then our moms are always "worried" about us and never stop with the reminders "to be aware of your surroundings." (Or is that just my mom?)

I have to say though, in all of my years of travel to various countries around the world, I have never found myself in danger. I'm not saying that women travelers never get into dangerous situations, but what I am saying is that it's not as common and widespread as you may think. If you're prepared, you'll feel more safe.

In this guidebook, I'll share the benefits of traveling solo and how it can help you deepen your connection to yourself and push beyond your self-imposed limitations.

I'll help you shift your mindset from anxiety to ease and confidence through affirmations and looking at traveling from a different perspective. Traveling solo means you're going alone, but you don't have to be lonely.

We'll talk about my experiences with different types of trips, like a staycation, weekend getaway, and domestic and international travel. You can always start small and then slowly expand your zone of comfort to places further from home.

If planning feels overwhelming, I have a whole chapter with sample itineraries for popular destinations that would be incredible choices for your first solo trip. I want to help you prepare for any adventure with ideas of where to go, what to pack, useful apps to utilize, and tips for staying safe. I have a knack for finding amazing restaurants, places to stay, and unique things to do in a given city. I've done all the research for you, so you don't have to.

My hope is that this book provides reassurance, guidance, and inspiration to overcome your fears and embrace the empowering experiences that await you!

1

EMBRACING THE SOLO JOURNEY
A GATEWAY TO SELF-DISCOVERY, ADVENTURE & PERSONAL GROWTH

"If you make friends with yourself you will never be alone."

– Maxwell Maltz

I had just finished a solo hike inside Kauai's Hā'ena State Park on the North Shore. When I return to my car, it happens to be farmer's market day in the parking lot. An unplanned surprise that I can't pass up.

I'm damp and chilled from a rainy day on the Nāpali Coast. I hold my yellow umbrella in one hand and a tote bag in the other. I'm overwhelmed with fresh produce options. The fruit looks much different than my local California market. I want to sample a bit of everything, so I buy one of each: the grapefruit, the guava, the star fruit. I wait in line for a while; no one is in a rush. Barefoot kids run around in the wet grass as their parents pay for fresh coconut drinks, ready to enjoy with long drinking straws.

My fruit loot has me feeling happy. Next, my eyes land on the Thai basil from the lady who grows it a mile up the road. The last stall sells buckets of bright flower bouquets filled with vibrant Bird of Paradise and palm fronds.

I could keep shopping, but I think this is enough to last for the few days I have left on the island. I pack up my goods and drive through the quiet town to my Airbnb.

As a first-timer to Hawaii, I chose Kauai solely because of this magical Airbnb. I often let accommodations dictate where I'll venture to. It's a fun backward way to end up in a place. The view from the main room is what dreams are made of. It's the quintessential Hawaiian landscape: lush green mountains, layers of fruit trees, and frequent rainbows painting the sky. At first, the sound of crowing roosters bothered me, but now it fades peacefully into the background.

On the worn wooden table, I slice open the grapefruit. It's juicy, sweet, and bitter as it hits my lips. Feeling content, I peer out the floor-to-ceiling windows, watching the heavy rain. I wrap up my afternoon snack with hot Thai basil tea.

I will never forget this day.

Benefits of Solo Travel

There are many benefits to traveling alone, but the three major ones I've found are experiencing a true sense of freedom, interacting with new people, and getting to know myself deeper.

Freedom

Think of all the travel you've done with family and friends. Everyone has their own wants and needs, so it's difficult to accommodate everyone's varying interests. Someone may want to marvel over Monets at the Met, and another is more into exploring ancient Egyptian relics at the Natural History Museum. Even if you travel with your partner, you might be ready to conquer the city, armed with a matcha latte and a dozen starred places on Google Maps, while your other half is pooped out by noon and dreaming of fluffy pillows and room service.

When you travel alone, none of that matters. You are the sole creator of your itinerary and get to do things that only appeal to you. No debating over where to eat. No rushing through a museum because your travel partner is bored. No compromises on early-morning hikes or late-night concerts. Every decision is yours, from where to go and what to see, to when to rise in the morning or call it a night. You get to dine where you please, spend as long as you want to admire that sculpture in the corner of the gallery, or change your plans entirely because you heard about a hidden gem from a friendly local.

You can go with the flow when you're alone. I love not overpacking my schedule to leave room for spontaneity. I check in with myself and ask, "What am I in the mood for today?" You can start with one thing on your wishlist, then see where the day takes you.

Meeting New People

When you first dip your toes into the solo travel pool, you might feel like you're wearing a neon sign that screams, "I'm all by myself!" You may be nervous about sympathetic glances from passersby, wondering why you're alone. In reality, these self-conscious thoughts are just figments of your imagination. Everyone's too absorbed in their own selfie-worthy moments to notice. If anything, they might be admiring the bravery of a solo traveler from a distance.

I'm something of an introvert, which is why solo travel first appealed to me. On a road trip several years ago, I stood near the edge of the Grand Canyon, surrounded by groups of tourists chatting and laughing. They were passing around cameras to take pictures of each other against the stunning natural backdrop, while I was pretty content in my own little world taking selfies.

However, if I wanted to capture a certain image that

8

my long arms couldn't manage, or felt like I missed human connection, I started chatting with people. Talking to strangers usually intimidates me, but I know that amazing things happen at the edges of your comfort zone. Sometimes this is as simple as asking someone to snap a photo of you.

There's magic in connecting briefly with another person in such a transient moment. You're sharing this unique experience with someone you otherwise have no ties to. In my experience, it's rare to initiate a conversation in that type of situation and get shut down. Most people are happy to share their amazement of the place you're in and get to know a little about your adventures.

I have also sat at the bar of a restaurant or a communal table and talked to people sitting by me. You'll likely meet a local and find great spots to check out—things you wouldn't learn from a guidebook. You might be surprised at what comes from these conversations. I've made friends who I stay in touch with even after I return back home.

Getting To Know Yourself

Before I started traveling, I thought I had a solid grasp of who I was. I understood my strengths and weaknesses, how I interacted with loved ones, and the activities that sparked joy in my everyday life. Little did I know that traveling alone would introduce me to a new version of myself. The moments spent in solitude, surrounded only by my thoughts, proved enlightening beyond measure. I make time to eliminate all distractions—even music, sometimes!— to truly listen to the inner workings of my mind and chart my next steps.

When I visit a new destination, I'm not just learning about the history of the place and the surrounding culture. I'm learning about myself. I'm finding out how I act in a new atmosphere. I notice things about the area and see how they impact me, what they make me think about, and how they make me feel. I used to think people moved to tears by a natural landmark were being dramatic, but then it happened to me. It was over-whelming in the best way possible.

You can explore various facets of your personality in a new place. No one knows you, so why not go for it? You can push yourself to pretend you're incredibly outgoing and confident, even if shyness is your usual disposition. You could play up the side of yourself that loves to be mysterious. You can tell people your name is your nick-name or your middle name to see how it feels. You could wear a wig. Travel is already an adventurous experience, so have fun with it while you get in touch with all aspects of yourself.

After many years of solo travel, you'd think that I'd be tired of all this alone time. But solitude allows for the chance to think, observe, and reflect. My perspective and outlook on the world is constantly evolving.

I love to begin or end each day by journaling. It helps my mind, heart, and soul process everything. Here are some travel-related prompts to get you started:

Write about your initial impressions when you arrive in a new place. What surprised you? What felt familiar?

Describe the place you're visiting using all five senses.

Note any cultural differences between your home and the location you're visiting.

Write about a memorable meal. Where was it? What made it special?

Did you meet someone who left an impression on you? What was their story?

Write about a hidden gem you discovered during your travels—a place off the beaten path.

If money were no object, what would you do if you could spend a day doing absolutely anything in the location you're visiting?

Sometimes the most memorable experiences are those

that weren't planned. Write about a spontaneous adventure you had.

What were your favorite experiences on your journey? Would you change anything?

Break Out of Your Comfort Zone

New situations are the essence of solo travel. You're exploring new destinations, trying new food, experiencing different cultures, and talking to strangers.

Even though I am an experienced traveler, I still get anxious and uncomfortable at times. Case in point: I flew to Tulum, Mexico to finish writing this book. (And drink smoothies on the beach). I researched ahead of time to find the best way to get to my Airbnb from the Cancun airport. A three-hour bus ride was one option. An expensive taxi ride was another. I was tired and battling a headache when the plane touched down. Feeling irritable as I exited baggage claim, I was hollered at by dozens of tour guides and taxi drivers, all competing for my money and attention. Navigating an unknown airport can be a bit nerve-racking, especially when all you want to do is lay down and order room service. (If you're curious, I decided to take a taxi from a trusted airport vendor. It cost me $115 but felt worth it in the moment).

What's my point here? My point is that you must

push through your discomfort, and the part of your brain that says, "I need to figure this out" eventually kicks in. You make a decision to the best of your ability, and even if it isn't the perfect choice, you roll with it and know better for next time. As a result, you gain a sense of confidence. You can say to yourself, *hey, I did that.* I figured it out all on my own. And then you are more likely to venture into the land of the unfamiliar in the future.

You're going to face new experiences every day as a solo traveler. It can get draining when you don't have anyone there to depend on. You can't complain about something to your best friend or let your partner make the next few decisions because you're not in the mood. It's all on you.

These are the times when you rise up and realize how strong you really are—how adaptable we humans can be. You'll discover strengths you didn't know you had and develop resilience and flexibility. Each success builds confidence and makes you more comfortable with being uncomfortable.

Let's Recap:

- Try not to stuff your itinerary to the brim and leave room for spontaneity.

- Nobody thinks less of you for traveling alone. They probably admire your independence and bravery.
- Bring a journal to document your travels and reflect on your experiences. Write out first impressions, sensory details in a scene, or a hidden gem you discovered.
- If you're feeling uncomfortable, take a deep breath, don't be afraid to ask for help, and make the best decision based on your instincts. You don't have to be perfect—it's all a learning experience.
- You confront and overcome your fears whenever you leave your comfort zone.

2

OVERCOMING OBSTACLES WITH A POSITIVE TRAVEL MINDSET

NAVIGATING UNCERTAINTIES, FEARS & EXTERNAL PRESSURES

"You're braver than you believe, and stronger than you seem, and smarter than you think."

– A.A. Milne

11,645 miles covered, 74 days on the road, over 194 hours of driving time, 29 states visited, 48 beds slept in.

One such "bed" was the front seat of my trusty 2012 Jetta. It's day 59 of my great American road trip, and I roll up to Bridge Bay campground at Yellowstone National Park. $26.33 a night gets you enough space to fit an 8x8 foot tent and one vehicle.

At this point on my road trip, money is running thin. I've been throwing purchases on my credit card left, right, and center. I'm proud of myself for deciding to save a few bucks on lodging tonight, since I've been splurging on cozy Airbnbs for most of this trip.

I'm not exactly outdoorsy, and I don't own a tent or any camping gear. I hope that a reclined seat, my green blanket, and a pillow will keep me comfortable for the night. My laptop is fully charged, so I can watch *Lords of Dogtown* after the sun goes down.

I check in to the campsite and sign a waiver acknowledging that I understand grizzly bears are in the park. I'm not scared, but I also don't want to go to the bathroom by myself in the middle of the night. I opt not to invest in bear spray, for whatever reason.

As 8 p.m. rolls around, my movie is almost over, and I'm a bit restless. I already ate my very fancy dinner of a peanut butter and jelly sandwich. I'm not tired but pretty bored, uncomfortable, and honestly, cranky. I feel like a weirdo sleeping in my car alone as the neighboring campsites with families in RVs glance my way. Maybe I should go to sleep and get an extra early start in the morning.

So I try that. I toss and turn in the passenger's seat and eventually doze off. I wake up a few hours later, totally freezing. Even in the middle of June, the temperature drops into the 40s at night.

I'm bundled up from my beanie down to my fuzzy socks, but I have to turn on the engine to crank the heater. I can't keep the car running all night, so after I warm up, I turn off the power and see how long the heat will keep the car warm. This cycle continues throughout the night.

Car sleeping would not be my preferred lodging option for future visits to Yellowstone. But sometimes, you have to make the best of what you're working with.

Such is life.

Common Reasons for Putting Off Solo Travel

The idea of solo travel is exciting, but it's not uncommon to wonder if it's actually a good idea. You're probably thinking, "Is this safe? Will it be too expensive? Can I really do this on my own?"

It's natural for these thoughts to arise. Your brain is trying to protect you. Your upbringing and society have shaped how your mind works, for better or worse. But we can learn how to shift our mindset so that nothing stops us from living the life we aspire to.

In this chapter, we'll address common objections to traveling alone. From concerns about financial limitations to fears of staying safe and experiencing loneliness, we'll delve into each objection and provide insights to overcome them.

Objection #1 - "I don't have time" or "I have to work"

Simple question: Do you love your life? If yes, amazing. If not, are you working on making changes? I truly believe that we can design the life we imagine for ourselves. Never settle. Life isn't about trading all your time for dollars and working 24/7 until you die.

While work is a crucial aspect of our lives, it doesn't have to be all-consuming. Numerous studies have shown the benefits of taking a break from work, not only for our physical health but also for our mental and emotional health. Taking time off allows for much-needed relaxation and boosts productivity when we return.

Though overworking is a phenomenon in many countries and across genders, women have added pressure because we are taught to always care for others and be selfless. In the workplace, we may not even consider our needs because we are so focused on what others need from us. Guilt arises when we consider taking time off instead of sticking around to help our co-workers get everything done.

I have to throw in an obvious travel analogy here. They say it on every airline: "In the case of an emergency, always put on your oxygen mask first before helping others." It's true. Remember that you must take care of yourself before effectively caring for the people in your life. This sentiment is true with work, friends, family, and romantic partners.

The idea that traveling takes a lot of time is not necessarily true. You don't have to fly halfway across the world. It could be as simple as exploring a new town over the weekend or going on a day trip. Even brief getaways give us a chance to recharge amidst our hectic schedules.

The key is to be intentional about setting aside time for these trips, just like you would for any other important task or meeting. If we don't prioritize travel, it will get pushed to the "someday" section of our to-do list.

Nicola Jane Hobbs says, "Instead of asking, 'Have I worked hard enough to deserve rest?' I've started asking, 'Have I rested enough to do my most loving, meaningful work?'"

Objection #2 - "I don't have the money"

The way we speak to ourselves affects our reality. Even a slight perspective shift could change everything. For example, instead of saying, "I can't afford this," ask yourself, "HOW can I afford this?"

Jen Sincero wrote a great book called *You Are a Badass at Making Money*. She pushes you to question where your beliefs about money come from. Do you have a scarcity mindset or one that welcomes abundance?

With that said, I know you probably also want some practical tips. The cost of travel ranges depending on your preferences. It doesn't have to cost thousands of dollars. In any event, you may need to set aside some savings before setting sail.

I love what financial guru Ramit Sethi says about spending. He advises ruthlessly cutting expenses on the things you don't care about and spending guilt-free on what you value most. For example, I don't like drinking very much. I'm not called to order a fancy cocktail at dinner and prefer not to spend my money on alcohol. However, I spend a pretty penny on takeout because cooking is not my thing. I try not to feel guilty about that, especially if I order healthy food that nourishes me.

Another way to lower your expenses is to challenge yourself to a year of no shopping. Does a year sound too extreme? Start with three months and see how it goes. I did this back in 2018. No new clothes, books, home decor, souvenirs when traveling, nothing...for a whole year. I even asked people not to buy me any birthday or Christmas gifts. At the time, I was trying to cut my spending, but I also liked the philosophical challenge of the experiment. Does *stuff* make us any happier? Buying a new pair of shoes may give us a temporary high, but then the excitement fades, and we are looking for the thing to get our fix. Everything is never enough.

We'll talk more about money in Chapter 4.

Objection #3 - "I'm scared" or "It's not safe"

There is a perceived danger of visiting foreign countries alone as a woman. When you think about it, any place can be scary or dangerous if you don't exercise a certain degree of caution. There are areas of my own city where I wouldn't walk alone after dark. Researching ahead of time can impact how anxious or calm you feel when traveling solo.

My biggest piece of advice is to avoid adopting a fear-based attitude. Fear mentality is driven by anxiety, insecurity, or a sense of impending threat. Maybe you have an intense fear of change or failure, or constantly worry about loss or not having enough. It's a self-protective mechanism. However, when left unchecked, it can lead to a restrictive life where you miss out on growth opportunities. In contrast, a growth mindset focuses on the potential for personal development and views setbacks as opportunities for learning and improvement. It's all about the way you look at it.

Let's say I'm flying to Amsterdam, and the airline loses my luggage. (By the way, this would be a bummer no matter how you look at it. But our reaction and inner dialogue could go in two different directions). A fear mentality says, "Terrible things like this always happen to me! I knew I should have never tried to take this trip alone—bad idea. Now I have to figure this out by myself. And curse you, United Airlines!" A positive mindset would spin it like this, "Well, what an interesting turn of events. This is an opportunity to overcome a challenge on my own. Glad I got trip insurance, so this will be covered. And now I get to go shopping!"

Overcoming fear-based thinking involves challenging deeply ingrained beliefs and developing healthier, more optimistic thought patterns. Take a close look at how you talk to yourself.

In the next chapter, we will go into more detail about how to stay safe as a female traveler, including some especially safe destinations and countries you may want to think twice about traveling to.

Objection #4 - "I'll get lost" or "Navigating a new place overwhelms me"

The current age we live in is prime time for traveling the world. Never before has there been so much access to resources and technology. The Internet provides an endless amount of information. Travel blogs, review sites, Pinterest, Instagram, Youtube, and TikTok offer insights and advice about destinations worldwide. If you want to do something, another person has already done it and is likely willing to share all their secrets. Planning trips, avoiding common mistakes, and discovering off-the-beaten-path destinations are easier than ever.

Smartphones have added a new level of convenience to travel. Flight and hotel booking, navigation, and language translation can all be done on the phone we carry with us everywhere. We can find the best places to eat, visit, and stay, all with just a few taps on a screen. This is such an incredible advancement from decades of the past!

Objection #5 - "It's going to be so lonely out there"

Many women worry about loneliness if they were to venture out on their own. It's a common concern, so don't let it make you feel like you're dependent on others. After all, think of how often you're alone in your daily life. Perhaps you live with family or roommates. You might have a significant other to go out with. You're around coworkers all day at work. You're always connected to others with your phone, social media, and emails. Many of us don't spend much time alone most days.

But when you travel, you're not just alone—you're alone in a new place. It's an unsettling situation until you learn to embrace it. Honestly, the first day is usually the hardest. You're going to be exhausted from the long journey. Once you give yourself a chance to unwind and get all the stress of the initial journey off your shoulders, your mood begins to shift.

If any fears arise, let them out with a short cry or another form of release. Know that the feelings will pass. Maybe go out for a drink or splurge on room service to lift your spirits. Or just hit the hay early and begin again tomorrow.

There's a major difference between being lonely and being alone. Of course you're alone—that's the very definition of solo travel! But being lonely is a state of mind. Loneliness arises from a sense of lacking. You're not with your family, friends, or partner, and you may be focused on the things you *don't have* at the moment. Try to shift your focus to what you are gaining from this alone time.

Loneliness typically arises as a result of something you didn't choose. Remember that you planned this trip and *wanted* to go solo, so you're in charge of this journey. You don't need to imagine what it would be like if your best friend was with you because that was never the plan. Focus on fostering your confidence and independence to move through feelings of loneliness.

If you start to feel more lonely than alone, remind yourself of the reasons you booked the trip. You most likely wanted to see something new and have time away from your daily life. You're giving yourself space to focus on yourself and explore your thoughts. It's legitimate to feel lonely at times. There will be good and not-so-good days, so let yourself experience all of your emotions.

Different people have various thresholds for alone time. Some people are very social and hate feeling cut off from their tribe. They might only feel comfortable traveling for a few days before they wish they were back with their circle. This is totally fine! You don't have to book a week-long journey to consider yourself a solo traveler. You can take long weekend trips and return to your friends for quality time together. Or if you find you love being alone, take a long summer trip. There's no wrong way to travel, so don't feel like you have to stay on the road longer than you can handle.

Once you start to embrace being alone, you'll realize how positive it truly is. Being alone lets you think your thoughts and feel your feelings without interruption. It allows you to recharge your brain and feel more empowered to support your loved ones when you return home. Your friends and family will see how each trip changes you and fully support your travels instead of saying things like, "Aren't you scared of traveling alone?"

Here are some positive mantras to help you lean into solitude:

- *Solo travel gives me the chance to learn about myself.*
- *I am my own best friend.*
- *I thoroughly enjoy my own company.*
- *I am savoring this alone time.*
- *Today I lovingly release feelings of loneliness.*
- *I welcome peace and quiet.*
- *Everything I need is within me.*
- *I am so happy to be doing this for myself.*
- *Time alone allows me to reflect and go inward.*
- *I take time for myself to recharge.*

Objection #6 - "Other people's opinions are deterring me"

Not everyone will understand or support your decision to travel, especially if it falls outside their comfort zone or perception of what is "normal." They might question your travel plans simply because they have a difference in perspective. If a person has never traveled before, their concerns are most likely based on fear of the unknown. And then they project these worries onto you. Their limited understanding should not define your reality!

I love the saying, "Don't take advice from someone you wouldn't switch places with." Always consider the source and remember that at the end of the day, it's your life, decisions, and experiences.

Parents often voice concerns about traveling solo because of their inherent instinct to protect you. Their apprehension comes from a place of love, so assure them that you are prepared. Share your plans, what you've learned about the destination through your research, and how you'll handle potential challenges. Hopefully that will help alleviate their anxieties.

Another question people love to ask is how you can afford all this--that's my favorite uninvited question. Your financial decisions are completely personal, and you don't have to answer that question if you don't want to. I have to remind myself that most people ask these money-related questions out of curiosity and don't intend to offend.

My final piece of advice is not to let unfounded fears or the limiting beliefs of others dictate your travel dreams.

Affirmations to Retrain Your Brain

Affirmations are short phrases that vocalize your mission and intentions, putting your truth into the universe. Thinking or speaking affirmations keeps these intentions at the forefront of your mind, and you'll soon realize how your attitude and actions change. They can shift your perspective and lead you through your journey with a positive mindset. They are perspective shifters.

Admittedly, it's easy to get bogged down in negativity. You may be nervous about taking a trip alone, and people around you are possibly perpetuating those anxious thoughts. Using affirmations helps push away unnecessary negativity, so you can prime your brain for positivity that will continue throughout your travels.

So how do we create these magical, life-changing affirmations? Start by imagining an upcoming trip and pinpoint any areas of anxiety. Are you worried about the flight? Securing a place to stay? Does the unknown terrify you? Write down all troublesome thoughts to find an affirmation for each of them.

Create your affirmations by flipping your worries into positive statements. For example, suppose you're worried about safety in a new city. You can say, "I feel safe because I stay aware of my surroundings," or "I'm a smart girl, and I know how to follow my instincts." If you repeat this every day (or several times a day!) before your trip, you'll start to believe the truth in the statement and feel more confident about your upcoming adventure. You can say affirmations aloud or write them in a journal.

Sometimes things don't go as planned. On a recent trip to Tulum, I was really cranky one day. I was riding around on my scooter in the intense heat, trying to locate the only vegan taco joint in town. I was uncomfortable from the dozen mosquito bites on my legs and the sweat trapped under my clothes. Google Maps was being inaccurate, so I was confused and frustrated. Finally, I found the taco place only to discover it was closed for no apparent reason. Since I'm human, my initial reaction was to complain or even start to tear up a little. (I know, a tad dramatic, but I was very hungry). But I pulled myself together and said something like, "I'm still adjusting to this new city. I can figure this out." I chose an alternative restaurant, and though the day didn't pan out as I envisioned, I reminded myself that everything doesn't have to be perfect all the time. Acceptance is key. I could turn this experience into an affirmation with something along the lines of, "I accept things as they are."

There are many other travel-related mantras. Consider starting with something from this list as you begin your journey. Over time, you'll have no trouble creating custom mantras to keep your spirits high no matter what situations you encounter on the road.

- *I'm grateful to have the opportunity to travel.*
- *I worked hard to plan and save for this trip, so it will be a great experience.*
- *I love having a chance to explore the world.*
- *I'm ready for new experiences in new locations.*
- *Every trip creates more memories.*
- *I appreciate the chance to get away from my daily routine.*
- *Traveling helps me live my life to the fullest.*
- *Taking a trip is self-care.*
- *Traveling makes me feel peaceful, successful, and accomplished.*
- *I appreciate the journey as much as the destination.*
- *I release my anxiety about traveling and embrace new experiences.*

Affirmations help calm your nerves and switch from finding negativity in every scenario to seeing hope in the potential of your trip. But you shouldn't judge yourself for the initial anxiety. At times, I still feel anxious on trips, so it's never something that completely goes away.

But get this—anxiety can actually be a good thing! It's your brain thinking of every possible situation and trying to solve problems before they happen.

Keep in mind, though, that most of the things you worry about will never happen. A study published in *Behavior Therapy* revealed that roughly 90% of our fears and worries never come true (Fielding, 2019). Worrying is part of being human, but remind yourself there is a big difference between your anxieties and reality.

If you feel inspired to start working with affirmations, I wrote an entire audiobook dedicated to travel affirmations. It includes one hour of audio that you can listen to anywhere—on the plane, in the car, or as you drift off to sleep at night. *Powerful Affirmations for Travel: Retrain Your Brain to Focus on the Positive, Ban Negative Self-Talk, and Build Confidence as You Travel the World* is available on Audible.

Coping Strategies When You're Feeling Low

Affirmations are a great tool to mentally prepare for traveling, but that isn't the only solution for moving through tough times. You can also leave some room in your budget for treats to pull yourself out of a funk if you feel down.

For example, I love good food, and I love not cooking. So I may treat myself to room service. The luxurious feeling of having food delivered to my door and eating while I'm kicked back on a comfy bed in my pajamas can't be beat! It always makes me feel better because I don't have to push myself to go out, but I still enjoy a delicious meal.

What makes you feel happy when you're traveling? I have friends who like to buy a new book and save it for vacation. They escape into a new fictional world, and feelings of loneliness are washed away. One woman I met while traveling takes small gifts to open on her trips. Sometimes she'll save a present from a recent holiday and pack it in her bag to open when she feels melancholy or disconnected. Or she'll buy something, wrap it, and hide it away so she forgets what's inside until she opens it on a trip. She eventually told people about this trick, and now friends will give her little trinkets to pack in her suitcase! She loves how the excitement of opening a gift lifts her spirits, and having something from a loved one brings feelings of connection.

Buying thoughtful souvenirs for friends and family is another great way to feel more connected to the people back home. When you return from your travels, they'll feel cherished that you thought of them while you were away.

Another pick-me-up idea is to write yourself a letter anytime before leaving for your trip and seal it in an envelope. Tuck it somewhere in your bag, and open it on the road when you need words of encouragement. Mine would read something like this:

Dearest Katherine,

How is the brave world traveler doing? I'm proud of you for setting sail on yet another adventure. That takes a lot of courage. Wanted to remind you to push yourself out of your comfort zone. Try complimenting a stranger or asking for recs on the best coffee spot in town. Remember, you can be anyone you want to be in this new place. Be daring.

Love, Me

Sometimes picking a new mantra helps me feel rejuvenated and confident. Or re-reading one of my favorite books from my shelves at home. If you feel overwhelmed or worn out while traveling, taking an afternoon off to nap can feel like a luxury, and it doesn't cost a thing.

Let's Recap:

- Reassess societal pressures to constantly be productive.
- Challenge yourself to a year of no shopping— this can lead to a greater understanding of personal happiness beyond material things.

- Rather than thinking, "I can't afford this," ask yourself, "How can I afford this?" Reflect on your money mindset. Is it one of scarcity or abundance?
- NOW is the time to travel! Technology and online resources make it easier than ever before.
- Identify your travel anxieties, jot them down, and create positive affirmations to address each concern.

3

SOLO AND SAFE

AWARENESS & PREPARATION ARE KEY

"Always let your conscience be your guide."
– Jiminy Cricket, *Pinocchio*

"Keep all the doors closed when you leave the room so wildlife can't come inside," the young Balinese man dressed in beige linen informs me as he drops my bags at the foot of the bed.

I nod in agreement and thank him for the warm welcome. Walking onto the balcony, I inhale the salty, warm air and feel immense gratitude for the ocean view. I sleep beautifully that night.

The following day I wake up naturally, without my usual 8 o'clock alarm. My favorite three words during any hotel stay are *breakfast is included*. I slip on my orange shorts and an oversized button-up, and head down to the open-air cafe. Something in my smoothie makes it a vibrant shade of magenta; must be the dragon fruit.

My fair skin can only take so much sun, so I stroll back to my room to get ready for the rest of the day. As I enter the room, I am shocked and initially delighted to see what I now know is called a Macaque monkey, known to the people of Bali as "Monyet," perched on the wood railing of the outdoor terrace.

Upon further inspection, I notice that it's holding something. Playing with it. Tearing it to pieces. I cautiously step closer to examine its toy.

"Oh dear...oh no!" I exclaim to myself.

The mischievous creature has gotten a hold of my wallet. Yep, the wallet with all my cash, ID, and credit cards. While I was leisurely sipping my smoothie, the Macaque managed to enter the room through the open sliding glass doors, find my purse, and retrieve the most valuable item he could find.

Perhaps I can reason with the monkey. I extend my arm.

"Give it to me!"

He backs away and grips the wallet tighter. One false move and my entire wallet will fall right into the Indian Ocean. There's no one around to help me, and I start to panic. I remember that I have a piece of chocolate in my bag. Maybe the monkey will be open to a trade. As I show him the treat, he looks suspicious. I don't think he is going to accept my peace offering. He scurries along the banister and hops onto the roof of a neighboring structure. He's getting away.

"Noooo! Mr. Monkey, come back!"

I desperately toss the chocolate bar on the roof, which draws him back in. He releases the wallet. My heart rate is at an all-time high. The chocolate has officially won over the monkey's attention. He nibbles at the edges and runs off into the trees with his new prize.

Victory! I blaze into the hallway looking for assistance, where I see the kind Balinese man in beige linen sweeping the hallway. I briefly recap my predicament. He uses the long-handled broom to scoop my wallet off the roof back to safety.

He smiles at me, knowing I must have forgotten his advice to keep all the doors closed. Lesson officially learned. Monkeys steal wallets. My room's going into lockdown from here on out.

Many women are eager for solo travel but are concerned for their safety. This is a common worry, and it shows that you're thinking clearly and looking ahead to protect yourself. But before spending your entire travel budget on new devices and tracking subscription plans, please know this chapter isn't meant to scare you! These tips give you an idea of the options available to keep you informed. Don't feel like you need every hotel door lock on the market or that you're obligated to stick to your exact itinerary so your family will know where you are at any given moment. Overall, the world is a safe place, and most people are well-intentioned and kind-hearted!

Research Your Destination: Checking Reputable Sources Before You Plan a Trip

Research is one of the most important safety measures. Instead of getting your information from media stories and hearsay from random people, use trusted websites based on research with your safety in mind.

The U.S. State Department is a great resource, even if you live outside the United States. Under their website's "Countries and Areas" list, you'll find travel information on visas, embassy locations, and recommended vaccinations. (Please note that visa and passport requirements vary based on your home country. More information on passports and visas can be found in Chapter 8).

Check out the current travel advisories that rate countries from level 1 to 4, depending on how safe it is to travel there. For instance, as I write this, France has a Level 2 Travel Advisory, which means "Exercise Increased Caution." The reasons for this are terrorism and civil unrest. If a country is rated with a Level 2, that doesn't mean you can't travel there. It is simply meant to alert you of potential safety issues so you are aware. These ratings can change at any time, so check back often. Here are the travel advisory levels:

1 - Exercise normal precautions

2 - Exercise increased caution

3 - Reconsider travel

4 - Do not travel

View the US State Department's country directory at state.gov/countries-and-areas-list. This fantastic resource will also refer to other sites if you want to be more thorough.

U.S. residents can enroll in The Smart Traveler Enrollment Program (STEP), a free program for those traveling or living abroad to register their trip with the nearest Consulate. Go to step.state.gov/step to create an account and sign up.

Other countries, like the Government of Canada, also have excellent travel advisory sites. Check out travel. gc.ca/travelling/advisories for more information on the specific country you are considering traveling to.

One last site to check out is the Centers for Disease Control and Prevention (CDC), which provides extensive information on recommended vaccines and other travel health notices, such as the quality of the drinking water. Read about your travel destination by visiting cdc.gov/travel.

Further Considerations for Selecting Your Destination

Though I think government-related travel advisories provide adequate information, further reports and studies are available if you'd like to dive deeper. An example of one such report is Georgetown University's *Women Peace and Security Index*. They measure women's justice, security, and inclusion in 170 countries. According to their 2021-2022 report, Norway, Iceland, Austria, Denmark, Sweden, and the Netherlands are among the top performers.

Though these are safe destinations overall, there can be a lot of variation within each country. I'll use the United States as an example, as I've lived here my whole life and traveled it extensively. We would never apply a blanket statement saying the *entire* U.S. is safe or unsafe. It's more nuanced and specific than that. Even declaring that a whole state is safe or unsafe would be too general of a statement. Crime rates and safety levels vary quite a bit depending on the city or even a neighborhood within a city. For instance, I feel entirely safe if I'm strolling beachside on a summer day in Santa Monica. On the flip side, if I am walking downtown in a heavily populated homeless area like Skid Row at night, I would feel very nervous and unsafe. Every country has safe and dangerous aspects, so the best advice is always to exercise caution, be aware of your surroundings, and follow common-sense safety practices regardless of your destination.

Trust Your Gut

You've done your research and feel equipped with the knowledge to stay safe and aware. The simple rule to follow is to trust your intuition. When making decisions, reflect on your inner feelings, hunches, and gut reactions. Sometimes, our subconscious mind can process information faster and more accurately than our conscious mind.

Street Smarts

Safety starts with being aware of what's going on. Keep your head up, eyes wide, and take everything in. Make eye contact, and don't be afraid to use your voice if you're scared or uncomfortable. This approach shouldn't make you feel paranoid, just aware.

It would be best if you also kept your ears open. Listening to music and letting your mind wander while exploring a new city or taking in a majestic view can feel magical. But I keep my earbuds tucked away when I'm strolling the streets. Then, I can hear the excitement of everything around me—the hustle and bustle of the local marketplace with vendors calling out to customers, the noise of honking horns, and children chattering in a foreign language.

At home or abroad, I limit my alcohol intake. Though a drink is nice here and there, too many can impair judgment and lower inhibitions. I want to stay alert and aware of my surroundings. Additionally, I try to do most of my adventuring during the day so I won't be walking alone at night. Sometimes, an outing takes longer than expected, and I'm out late. In that case, I may opt to take an Uber back to my hotel.

You might consider carrying pepper spray in your bag or on your keychain. Although I have never needed to use it, it does give an added sense of security. Pepper spray is actually illegal in some countries, but travel-size hair spray or bug spray are alternatives. You'll get double duty from an item you'd pack anyway, so it's easy enough to throw in your everyday bag.

Let's touch on a few money-related tidbits. Thieves will target unaware tourists in crazy ways. They may approach you requesting a donation or asking you to sign a petition to get close enough to steal your valuables. This has not happened to me, but keep it in the back of your mind if the situation presents itself. Always keep an eye on your purse, making sure it doesn't hang open off your shoulder or leave it out of sight on the back of your chair.

Lastly, do not feel pressured into buying something you don't want. In tourist spots, sometimes it's hard to turn down persistent vendors. They may even try to employ questionable sales techniques like using kids to lure you in or tying a bracelet around your wrist and then insisting that you purchase it—a simple "no thank you" and a kind smile usually do the trick. And then walk away.

Safety Gadgets and Apps

While this isn't specifically a safety app, posting on social media can keep you secure. You don't need to advertise where you are if you have public accounts, but you can check in and post something on Twitter, Facebook, Instagram, or TikTok to show your loved ones that you're okay. If you have a private account, you can always share pictures and notes about your day or post about your plans for the next day. This allows people to keep tabs on you without you needing to spend time calling, texting, or emailing several different people.

I suggest downloading the app Life360 so you can share your location and whereabouts with someone back home. I have a free account, but you could consider a paid version for the time when you'll be traveling. Parents use the app for teens with their first taste of independence with cell phones and driver's licenses. It tracks their locations and driving speeds and sends crash alerts if necessary. When you understand how the app helps parents track teens, you can see how it's a great idea for women traveling alone in a distant location.

If you're an Apple fan, you'll love how seamlessly Bluetooth AirTags integrate with your devices. Keep one on your keychain and press the button to locate your purse, backpack, or suitcase if you get separated from them. If you're a Mac user, ensure the "Find My" feature is enabled on your phone and computer. It will track the location of your laptop, phone, AirPods, and other devices. Find My also has location-sharing features, similar to what I mentioned with Life360.

Google Maps is a game changer for travel. It allows me to see what public transportation will take me to specific destinations and provides walking directions. You can also look at street views of each destination to ensure you'll recognize it when you see it in person. If you're on a road trip, Google Maps will give you the option of driving on highways for a quick journey or back roads for a scenic drive.

In addition to apps, there are some devices and gadgets you can pack to ensure you feel safe wherever you are. Portable door locks almost seem like overkill to me, but if it makes you feel more secure, it's an easy and inexpensive item to pack. When you close your hotel or Airbnb door, you put the lock between the jamb and the door. It keeps the deadbolt in place, so no one can get inside until you come to the door and remove it.

Personal alarms attach to your backpack strap like a

keychain or fit comfortably in your pocket. They have a small button on the case that you can press when you need help or feel in danger. The alarm is so loud you won't believe it comes from such a tiny device. It will scare away anyone who mistook you for an easy target while drawing the public's attention to what's going on.

If you're staying in a shared accommodation like a hostel, luggage locks secure your zippers so no one can open your bag and rifle through your belongings. You can purchase old-school locks that require a key, use a combination lock, or splurge on more technical locks that use your fingerprint.

How to Dress

When traveling, I want to express myself with fashion, but I also don't want to be a target—as a stereotype for Americans is that they are all wealthy. For this reason, you may think twice about wearing expensive jewelry or other flashy items. I still bring nice things while I travel, but I usually don't pack anything I would be devastated to lose.

Do a bit of research on how women dress in your destination. Respect norms and be aware of how more conservative cultures dress. You don't want to call attention to yourself by wearing shorts and a tank top if women usually cover up on the streets. This approach is especially important if you're visiting religious landmarks. Countries with a prominent Muslim, Hindu, or Buddhist influence are often the ones where you'll need to show less skin. Covering your knees and shoulders is considered respectful, so it's nice to have a scarf to wrap around you if needed (Rich, 2023).

Stay Connected

Maintain regular communication with someone you trust back home. Share your travel plans, itinerary, and important contact information with them. Regular check-ins provide a sense of security and ensure someone knows your whereabouts.

Have an emergency plan. Write down information about police stations, hospitals, and similar safe places for each destination during your journey. You'll have the information at your fingertips if you need it instead of stopping and looking things up while you're there.

Transportation

Figuring out transportation in a new place is one of the trickier aspects of travel, especially if it's a different mode of transport than what you're used to at home. Here is an overview of the different ways to get around:

Public Transit

Many destinations, like New York City or popular European cities, have excellent public transportation options. Their subway systems make it easy to get from point A to point B. I have to admit I'm not intuitively good with directions. I haven't always felt confident when it comes to figuring out where I'm going, but that all changed when I started using Google Maps. It tells you exactly which trains, buses, and metro lines to take to get where you need to go. (Make sure to bring a portable phone charger, so your phone doesn't die when you're out and about and you have no idea how to get home).

Trains are among my favorite modes of transport. In Germany, I took a train from Cologne to Berlin. It was a leisurely four hours spent reading, listening to music, and gazing out the window. Sometimes, I get nervous when the ticket examiner comes by and asks to see my ticket. I fear that one of these days, he'll say, "You're not on the right train. This isn't the correct ticket. You have to get off at the next stop." But that has never happened. Before the train departs, I usually check in with another passenger and ask something like, "This train is going toward Berlin, right?"

Some places in the world may not have the best public transportation. For instance, the metro system in Los Angeles is not very extensive, and it doesn't feel particularly safe to me. There are some questionable folks on there. (At least, that was the case the one time I took the A-Line downtown on New Year's Eve). Take note of the kinds of people that are on buses and subways. If there are women and children onboard, that gives me a hint that it is safe. I'd suggest researching public transit in your specific destination to ensure it's a safe and common way to get around.

Taxis & Ubers

Consider trusted and licensed sources; don't just take a ride from anyone. Taxis have always made me a little nervous because it's hard to tell if you're getting ripped off, especially if there is no meter in the cab. You could have your hotel arrange transportation so you are sure to get a fair price. Show the driver the address of your destination and know the price before you get in the car. Also, confirm that they accept credit cards if you plan to pay that way. From my experience, taxi drivers will likely prefer cash.

I mentioned I might take an Uber if I'm out at night. Not every location has Uber drivers, but if they do, I prefer this service to local taxis. The app keeps data about your location and the driver, plus you don't have to worry about paying the driver directly since payment methods are stored in the app. If you're in a country like Indonesia, which does not have Uber, there may be similar apps like the Bluebird Group in Bali.

Renting a Car

If you have to drive far from the airport or stay in a more secluded area, a rental car may be your best bet. I like this option because it gives me the most freedom. I will say it's a bit nerve-wracking to rent a car in a foreign country. In New Zealand, I was driving on the opposite side of the road. In Paris, the traffic was bananas. But again, I go slow and try not to drive during peak traffic hours. I recommend using a trusted and well-known rental car service instead of a budget one. Budget rental services may appear cheaper upfront, but there could be hidden costs and fees or possibly poor customer support. Reputation and reviews are important when renting a car domestically or internationally. You may want to check out Discover Cars, an online car rental platform with upfront costs and free cancelation.

Scooters

I've rented a motorbike, sometimes called a scooter, in Thailand, Mexico, Bali, and Vietnam. I'd only recommend this if you feel comfortable and confident doing it, as it's not for everyone. I also don't mess around with attempting to drive a scooter in traffic. In my opinion, it's only enjoyable when you have a lot of open space and don't feel stressed about navigating around cars and crowds. It may take a day or two to get used to, but it's a fun way to get around if you go slow and avoid busy areas.

Walking & Biking

This is arguably the most lovely way to explore a new place. You can go at your own pace, slowly taking in all the sights and sounds. Not to mention, it's the most environmentally friendly.

Travel Insurance

Thankfully, I've never had any travel-related emergencies—not even lost baggage or severe illness abroad. Perhaps I've just been lucky. I don't advise traveling without insurance because you will surely wish you had it if anything goes wrong and it could have been covered.

Travel insurance is protection against losing money for a canceled trip, missed flight, misplaced luggage, or illness. You can choose different policies to suit your needs.

If you get sick while overseas, your primary insurance policy might not cover your medical expenses, but travel insurance will. It also covers costs you might incur trying to replace lost luggage. Airlines rarely pay out when this happens, and they only consider your bag lost after 21 days. Travel insurance will reimburse you for what you lost.

People who worry they might need to cancel a trip at the last minute will benefit from travel insurance. Maybe you have a trip planned, but a loved one has health issues, and you want the opportunity to stay close if necessary. Most hotels and airlines require at least two weeks' notice and may charge cancellation fees. Travel insurance offsets this expense, so you won't lose money when canceling a trip.

Many standard insurance companies offer travel insurance, so you can check with your provider and possibly get a discount by bundling services. You can also visit <u>WorldNomads.com/travel-insurance</u> for more information and reputable companies. I recently used Faye Travel Insurance, and I appreciated how straightforward and user-friendly it was. For two weeks in Tulum, it cost me $81.

Hiking & Outdoor Activities

Is it safe to hike alone? In most cases, yes. But it also comes with some risks and considerations. Take into account your level of expertise and the difficulty of the hike. The trail should be well-marked and well-traveled. Remote trails where there is no one around means that if you need help (for instance, if you slip and sprain your ankle), there may be no other hikers to assist you. Before you go on a solo hike, mention it to a friend or family member and give them an estimated time for when you will be done. You can send them your exact location (before you lose cell service) and provide emergency contact numbers just in case.

Another tip is to familiarize yourself with wildlife in the area and how to react if you encounter wild animals. Know the weather forecast and be prepared for extreme temperatures or storm warnings. Will there be an altitude change that is higher than what you're used to? Carry a mini first aid kit with some bandaids and antiseptic wipes. And pack plenty of water and snacks!

If all this overwhelms you, but you want to experience nature, consider going with a small group or an experienced guide.

LGBTQ+ Considerations

Sadly, not all countries are fully accepting of the LGBTQ+ community. LGBTQ+ friendliness varies across countries and even among different regions within a country. For example, even though the landscape is shifting from previous decades, the United States is not 100% accepting of the LGBTQ+ community. Some cities, like Portland, San Francisco, and many others, are progressive, while select areas in the south or midwest may be more conservative.

You may want to investigate your destination's social attitudes toward LGBTQ+ individuals. A great resource I found is Equaldex.com.

You could also connect with local LGBTQ+ organizations where you plan on traveling. They can provide support and insight into the community and suggest LGBTQ+ friendly spaces and events.

Let's Recap:

- Before planning a trip, check on the destination's current travel advisories.
- Get some travel insurance! It's good for peace of mind and potential emergencies.
- Share your travel plans, itinerary, and essential contact information with one or two people back home. Look into downloading the Life360 app or something similar.
- Consider what you do to stay safe in your home city—those same precautions will serve you well wherever you go.
- Regardless of your destination, stay aware of your surroundings and adopt common-sense safety measures.
- Above all, trust your intuition.

4

THE ONE ABOUT MONEY
ENJOY RICH EXPERIENCES

"Nothing behind me, everything ahead of me, as is ever so on the road."
— Jack Kerouac

I have fully embraced my inner hippie.

It's the summer solstice, and I'm in Tulum, Mexico. The hotel down the street is hosting a cacao and honey ceremony, and though I don't fully know what that entails, I sign up.

I gather around a large fire pit with about ten other spiritual souls. Our guide Michel speaks in a blend of English and Spanish. Everything he says in Spanish sounds more poetic and meaningful than its English translation. He wears his hair in a ponytail, and a pendant on a black string hangs around his neck.

The ceremony begins with Michel giving each of us a

piece of raw cacao. It tastes bitter. He tells us to toss the skin of the cacao bean into the fire pit.

We begin to move, stomp, dance, and flow. There are feathers, instruments I've never seen or heard before, incense smoke, and the scent of tobacco.

We close our eyes and breathe deeply.

"Inhalo...y exhalo." *Breathe in, breathe out.*

I try my best to remain present. Here I am, somewhere in the jungle on the Yucatan peninsula. The immense heat from the combination of the growing fire and the first-day-of-summer sun encourages beads of sweat to gather on my forehead.

We are handed a piece of paper and asked to write a letter expressing gratitude for our lives, as well as something we are ready to let go of. Michel tells us the Mayans believe that honey has healing powers and is a symbol of prosperity and vitality. He then drenches each of our notes with Mayan honey before we throw them into the fire.

As you prepare to dive into your upcoming adventures, there's a practical side that deserves attention: understanding the costs that accompany your travel dreams. That's where this chapter comes in. We'll walk through everything from calculating daily costs to snagging flight deals to tipping etiquette. My goal is to arm you with the skills needed to make your trip not only unforgettable but financially savvy too.

How Much is this Trip Going to Cost?

It's hard to say exactly how much money you'll need since this will obviously range depending on your accommodations, where you are going, and the length of your trip. You can roughly calculate a per-day cost, including expenses like accommodation, airfare, transfer to and from the airport, and food. Here are the main spending categories:

- **Transportation costs:** Flights (including add-ons like checked baggage), getting to and from the airport, and local transportation (Ubers, public transport, rental cars, etc.)
- **Lodging:** Include taxes and resort fees, which may not be listed until checkout.
- **Meals:** Consider your morning coffee, breakfast, lunch, dinner, snacks, and drinks. Estimate the cost of groceries if you cook some meals and eating out at restaurants.
- **Travel insurance and health costs:** Short-term travel insurance is usually charged per day. Health costs include vaccinations or special medications.

- **Daily activities:** Tours, museum entry, attractions, etc.
- **Spending money:** Shopping for souvenirs and local goods.
- **Currency conversion:** Account for exchange rates and potential fees when withdrawing cash or card transactions.
- **Miscellaneous:** Tips, visas, and unexpected expenses.
- **Buffer:** I like to add a 10% to 15% buffer to what I expect the total to be, just in case.

If you're a spreadsheet nerd like me, check out this handy *Trip Cost Calculator* I made just for you: bit.ly/trip-calculator

To spend money modestly, ask yourself what you value most when traveling. I appreciate nice lodging, but maybe all you need is a simple place to rest your head at night, and you would rather spend your money elsewhere.

If I feel like I'm spending too much money on a trip, I'll play the would you rather game with myself. For instance, here in Mexico, I was considering booking a coffee-tasting experience on Airbnb, but I also wanted to get a Mayan clay massage. Both were about the same price. The best-case scenario would be to do both, but if I'm tight on cash, I'll choose one or the other. Though I love purchasing physical keepsakes and souvenirs from around the world to remind me of my travels, I try to spend money on experiences over material things.

Setting Aside Money for Your Trip

You may want to consider opening a new bank account that you can put money into each month to save up for a trip, like a virtual piggy bank. I have a separate bank account nicknamed "Travel" that I transfer money into on an ongoing basis. You could do this manually whenever you have an extra few hundred dollars on hand or set up a recurring automatic transfer so that the money builds up without you even thinking about it. The easier you make it, the more likely you'll do it.

My final note here is to not let lack of funds discourage you and keep you from traveling. Think back to Chapter 2, where we talked about overcoming objections with a positive travel mindset. In previous years, I've struggled with finances and overspending. But I continue to remind myself that I can change at any time, and my past does not define my future. I can choose to struggle financially, or I can choose to be financially free. And I will always aim toward the latter.

Savings on Flights

One of the easiest ways to look for flights is on Google Flight Tracker, which helps you find the lowest airfare for your destination. Turn on the price tracker feature so that you get an email update whenever the price of a flight goes up or down. When you are ready to purchase, it will take you directly to the airline's website to book the ticket.

I kind of love the idea of letting cheap airfare decide where you go. Skyscanner has an "Explore Everywhere" feature. Enter flexible travel dates like "July 2023" and have the destination set to a specific country or even "Everywhere." If you're feeling spontaneous, peruse the site, and you may find a deal you cannot pass up.

Look closely and carefully at unusually low airfare prices since there may be hidden fees (like charging for seat selection or bringing a carry-on bag on board). Personally, I would only opt for a budget airline like Ryanair or Spirit on a short flight. TripAdvisor reviews reveal these types of airlines have less legroom, no in-flight entertainment, and possibly lower quality customer service. But if $81 could get you from Los Angeles to New Orleans, how much do you care about a little temporary discomfort? On the other hand, sometimes it's worth it to pay more for your ticket if it means departing at a favorable time of day and a nonstop flight.

One last tidbit of advice is to search for flights in a private web browser because cookies save your search history and may affect flight prices. I'm skeptical whether or not this is true, but I suppose it doesn't hurt to go incognito.

Savings on Lodging

You can either book directly on a hotel's website or use a third-party booking site. Try downloading the Expedia or Booking.com app on your phone, since they offer exclusive discounts to encourage people to use the mobile app. You may receive an extra 10% off your hotel stay by booking this way.

Design Hotels is my absolute favorite site for booking hotels. After you sign up (it's free), you can get a Community Deal of around 30% off stunning select hotels.

Airbnb offers discounts on weekly or monthly stays. I've had the most luck with finding great deals when I enter flexible travel dates. Nightly pricing fluctuates on many Airbnb rentals. You might be able to find a last-minute deal, as hosts sometimes lower prices to fill their calendars if the place is still available.

Payment Options Abroad

You'll want to use a credit card when traveling in certain situations, while others will require cash.

Cash

It can be stressful to touch down in a new country and not have any cash on hand. I wouldn't assume that credit cards will be accepted wherever you go, as some countries prefer to operate in cash. Relying on ATMs to withdraw cash at the airport can be risky. Sometimes they are broken, or have a maximum amount you can withdraw that is less than you need, or your debit card isn't working for whatever reason.

It's wise to arrive at your destination with about $200 cash in your home currency. You can exchange it for the local currency once you arrive. The exchange rates at airport kiosks are not the best, though I have exchanged money there in a pinch. Finding a bank to exchange money is a good option.

For any additional cash you need throughout your trip, the easiest way to obtain foreign currency is through an ATM once you get there. If your bank or the ATM charges you a fee, take out all the cash you need in one visit so you don't have to pay the fees multiple times. If possible, go for an ATM from a reputable bank instead of a privately owned one. Try to find a secure ATM, preferably inside a store or bank.

How much cash you need will depend on the country you visit. In South America, Mexico, and Southeast Asia, I've found that it's useful to always have cash on hand. On the contrary, in Europe, Australia, and Canada, there are a lot of cashless transactions where credit cards and digital wallets are widely accepted.

Debit & Credit Cards

It is generally recommended to inform your credit card issuer about your travel plans, especially if you are going to use your credit card in a foreign country or for significant purchases. This will help avoid your card from being declined when making purchases in an unrecognized new location. You can often inform your card issuer online or in their mobile app.

Credit cards that don't charge foreign transaction fees are ideal when making purchases abroad. A common foreign transaction fee is around 3%, so you'd be charged an additional $3 on a $100 purchase. It's not a substantial amount, but it adds up if you are using your card for every purchase. I'd suggest opting for a widely accepted credit card like VISA. I made the mistake of bringing my Discover card to Mexico (because it offers no foreign transaction fees) but quickly realized that Discover is not accepted everywhere. Many of my attempted purchases were declined and I had to pay with cash.

In addition to bringing one or two credit cards, you'll need a debit card in case you have to withdraw cash. It would be wise to have a backup card just in case your primary card gets flagged for fraud or is misplaced and you need to close it down. When possible, I prefer to use my credit card instead of a debit card, since credit cards provide stronger protection against fraud than debit cards tied to a bank account.

Tipping Protocol

If you go out for a meal, take a taxi, get a massage, or partake in any other service-based activities while you're away, you may be wondering whether tipping is expected and, if so, how much you should tip. Here are a few instances in which tipping might be recommended, depending on the country:

- Restaurants & bars
- Hotels - for assistance carrying bags, housekeeping, valet parking, or concierge services
- Guides, tours & drivers
- Massages, facials, or other pampering services

It would be tedious to list the expectations and customary tipping amounts for each country individually, but I'll provide a general overview of some different parts of the world. These recommendations focus on restaurant etiquette but keep in mind there are other situations in which tipping may be common.

In the U.S. and Canada, tipping is expected at restaurants, with anywhere from 15% to 25% being in the acceptable range. Honestly, my idea of when and how much to tip here at home in the U.S. is kind of warped. Because it is expected 100% of the time, I feel guilted into tipping generously and have forgotten how to base my tip on the quality of service provided. I've heard many times that servers, bartenders, and baristas depend on their tips because their wages are so low. I hope that is not the case in all countries.

In Mexico as well as in Central and South America, tipping is also commonplace. About 10-15% of the total bill is a good estimate of how much to tip.

Tipping percentages are slightly lower in Europe. Leaving a tip larger than 15% to 20% may be considered excessive. The Netherlands is actually one country that does not expect patrons to leave a tip since it is often included in the cost of the service. Even still, some people in the Netherlands add on a small 5% bonus for good service. Tipping is also not customary in other countries in the EU (European Union), such as France, Spain, and Sweden. However, if the service goes above and beyond, a small tip would be a generous token of appreciation. Leaving a generous tip is not customarily done in Ireland, Germany, the UK, or Portugal, so it is up to you to leave a gratuity. Unless there is a service charge included on the bill or the service was exceptionally poor, the general rule of thumb is to tip between 5% and 10% (Horowitz, 2017).

Tipping is not common practice in Asian countries

such as Singapore, China, and Japan. Some servers in Japan may even politely turn down your tip since great service is simply embedded into their way of life. In tourist areas of Thailand, Indonesia, and Vietnam, tips would be accepted but are not mandatory.

In Australia, the general view is that service industry employees are compensated well, hence tipping is not customary. Servers and drivers in Australia and New Zealand appreciate if you round up the bill, but do not expect tips.

As you can see, there are nuances to tipping in every country, so it's probably best to do a quick search online that is tailored to the exact destination you are going to. For instance, search "tipping etiquette in Costa Rica" to make sure you didn't overlook any important advice.

Let's Recap:

- Try setting aside money in a separate bank account if you're saving up for a trip.
- To get the best price on airfare, check out Google Flights and track prices for a few days or a few weeks.
- Check out Design Hotels Community Deals on some of the prettiest independent hotels.

- Bring a small amount of cash, 1-2 debit cards to withdraw from an ATM, and 1-2 credit cards for purchases.
- Check your bill to see if a tip (also known as gratuity or a service charge) is included in the total. If not, consider rounding up or leaving an extra 10-20% depending on where you are in the world.

5
_____

EXPLORING NEAR AND FAR

CONSIDERING THE MANY STYLES OF ADVENTURING

"Life shrinks or expands in proportion to one's courage."

– Anais Nin

The listing title caught my eye: "Gumbo Kinney Designer Glamper for Joshua Tree Stargazing." A 1957 trailer in the middle of the desert, just two hours from my home in Los Angeles. When I see a low price tag and some funky aesthetics, I click "book" pretty quickly. I may have overlooked that everything is off-grid, so the whole shebang is powered by solar and propane. Not difficult, but different.

At one point in time, I strongly considered purchasing my own slice of land in the desert and building a small cabin out there amidst the dust and Dr.

Suess-esque Joshua trees. So the '57 Spartan served as a base camp as I checked out acreage for sale.

At night it gets dark. Real dark. Unlike the city, the roads lack street lamps, and the only light comes from the dim shine of the moon. Once the sun goes down, I stay cozied up inside.

The trailer is long and skinny, with retro lime green dining chairs, curtained windows at one end, and a king-size bed at the other. At night in early March, temperatures drop low in the desert. I worry that I'll use up all the propane trying to stay warm, so instead, I bundle up under the covers wearing a sweatshirt and my infamous fuzzy socks. As I lay there, the wind starts to pick up, and the trailer sways from side to side.

I feel kind of alone out here in the windy desert. But I love the sense of adventure, and I love a good travel story.

My personal motto is *go big or go home*, but that advice doesn't give everyone the same thrill it gives me. There's no reason to push yourself *too* far out of your comfort zone when you are first getting started. I traveled over 4,000 miles from home on my first solo trip, but that's not the only way to start traveling alone. You can absolutely start small. This could look like a staycation in your own town or a destination that is only a couple of hours away. I'm including several different options in this chapter so you can choose one that captures your interest. Adapt these suggestions to best suit your budget, destination, and interests.

Staycation

A staycation is a short vacation to a place close to home. If you're not used to doing things on your own, this is a way to ease into solo travel. Some people love the experience of staying in a hotel for a night and exploring the area the day before and after checkout. Or you might choose to take several days off work and have a staycation that lets you explore the city for a weekend or longer.

I recommend booking a staycation in your city but staying away from home. For example, I live on the east side of Los Angeles. As silly as it sounds, east siders don't get over to the west side very often. It's only a 45-minute drive, but with traffic, it definitely feels like a trek. And so I present to you...the perfect staycation opportunity. For my birthday, I booked a one-night stay at the Proper Hotel in Santa Monica, a superb place to enjoy a side of LA I don't get to see often. New restaurants, new scenery, new crowds of people.

Staying at a hotel, bed & breakfast, or Airbnb will get you out of the house so you be a tourist in your own city. This means you're not grabbing a latte from your favorite café in the morning and going to the local bar to hang with your friends at night. You're going to explore a different area of town and try things you've never done before.

Many people live in a city for years without hitting the popular museums and tourist attractions. There are people in New York who haven't been to the top of the Empire State Building, people in Memphis who haven't toured Graceland, or even people in Arizona who haven't made it to the Grand Canyon. When you live somewhere, you tend to feel like you'll get around to such experiences eventually, but for now, you need to work, hang out with friends, and stick to your routine. A staycation removes those elements from the equation, freeing you up to see your city through a new lens.

If your own city doesn't excite you (it needs to excite you!) then look at neighboring cities an hour or two away. Once you have a city or town selected, look at the attractions, restaurants, and stores you've never been to. You might notice that many of them are in the same location, like several galleries and museums downtown. Maybe you choose to book a hotel downtown so you can walk or take public transportation instead of depending on your car. If your points of interest are scattered throughout the city, that works too. Driving your car gives you a lot of freedom to get where you need to go.

My favorite way to map out what I want to see and do in a new place is by starring places on Google Maps.

After I book my accommodation, I mark it as a favorite by clicking the "save" icon, so I can get a sense of the neighborhood I'm staying in. Then I click on the fork and knife icons (which indicate restaurants) to see what is close by. I also like checkout out on the coffee icons, which are cafés. If the place has 4.5 stars or higher, it captures my attention enough to take a closer look. I quickly scroll through the pictures and assess how tasty the dishes look, as well as the overall ambiance of the restaurant. If it passes my test, I will add it to my favorites. This is a great strategy because whenever I am out and about, I can quickly pull up Google Maps and see what starred places are close to me.

Weekend Getaway

Planning your first solo trip as a weekend getaway is a great way to dip your toes in the water without dedicating a lot of time and money to the cause.

You can start by booking your accommodations in a city or national park a few hours away from where you live. This gives you the ability to drive your own car and pack anything you need without worrying about the constraints of airline luggage. You'll most likely know a few things about the city already and have an idea of the weather so you can pick the right weekend and pack accordingly. Maybe a nearby city has an annual festival you've always wanted to experience, or your favorite band is playing at a venue there. Or maybe you don't have a reason to visit beyond it just being a close location that's worth exploring!

A weekend getaway gives you a chance to enjoy your own company. You can bring a book or a journal to dine solo in a restaurant. You'll have time to reflect on what you saw that day, everything you learned about a location's culture or history, and anyone you met and interacted with. You can also spend time thinking about what you'll do the next day and change up your itinerary if you learned about cool places during your time there.

Cabins & Cottages

My idea of fun is creating Airbnb wishlists for places to stay in different parts of the world. I've found dozens of cabins that are so stunning, they're a trip in themselves. I could spend a whole weekend in an A-frame cabin in the woods just hiking and staring at the way the light streams in a wall of windows. Peruse my curated wishlist, "Cabins for One" and see if any of these locations appeal to you: bit.ly/cabins-wishlist.

Some Airbnb cabins have record players or Bluetooth speakers, so play around with creating a playlist for the experience. You could book a cabin with a hot tub so you can relax with tea or wine. Many cabins have a full kitchen, including pots, pans, dishes, and utensils. You can stock up on food at the grocery store and spend your trip cooking meals for yourself. (Don't forget the snacks). If you don't like to cook, book a cabin that's not too far from civilization and go out for meals.

With this type of trip, you're able to disconnect from your busy life, commune with nature, improve your mood, and reconnect with what makes you feel alive. You could go for a leisurely walk, eat and read outdoors, go swimming, or bring along activities like crosswords, sudoku, or paint by numbers. If you feel like you haven't had time for a creative pursuit, now is your chance to remedy that. You can write, draw, paint, or create music without interruptions from other people or more pressing responsibilities.

Domestic Travel

Opt for more extensive domestic travel after you take a staycation or weekend getaway, or jump right in by visiting a new state that's been on your wish list for years.

When it comes to domestic travel, there are several benefits that set it apart from international travel. Firstly, domestic travel often involves shorter travel times, allowing you to reach your destination relatively quickly. You don't have to worry about long-haul flights or navigating complex international airports, making the journey smoother and less exhausting. It can be more cost-effective, as shorter flights are often less expensive. Another advantage of domestic travel is the familiarity with the culture and language. Being in your home country means you can easily communicate with locals and feel more at ease in your surroundings.

Planning a road trip is an amazing travel idea for deepening the connection to your own country. I once drove from California to Maine and back on a solo trip. I knew the United States had a lot to offer, but seeing so many different states opened my eyes to its rich history and diverse landscapes. By exploring your own back-yard, you gain a greater appreciation for the beauty within your own borders.

International Travel

International travel can feel daunting. The logistical aspects like planning, budgeting, navigating unfamiliar languages, and working through unexpected situations in a foreign country add to the intimidation factor. But fear not! I'm here to help you prepare.

When you're planning an international trip, start by researching countries that speak a language you know fluently. Your language may be English, something you speak at home, or a language you studied in school. Whatever language you feel confident speaking to order food, get directions, or ask for help is an option here. (You don't have to choose a country that speaks your language, but that makes your first trip considerably easier).

I like to have at least 10 days for international trips to adjust to the time difference and get situated. Keep in mind that two of those days will be designated travel days spent getting there and back. Don't put off international travel if you have less time available. For your first trip, if the flight isn't too long, something like 5 to 7 days may be ideal to test the waters and see how you like it.

Having an itinerary will help you feel like you're getting the most out of your travel experience. However, it's also important to build in some downtime to hang out in a café, talk to locals and fellow travelers, or try something you didn't plan for. Doing this will give you an idea of your travel style. You'll learn how flexible you are and whether you prefer knowing everything you'll do or only planning a few activities and then seeing what appeals to you once you're there.

Other Possibilities

The following ideas are for women who are looking for a more structured vacation or would to travel alongside a build-in community.

Organized Group Tours for Solo Travelers

If you're not sold on the idea of heading off by yourself, consider a planned group tour. Under 30 Experiences and the Solo Female Travel Network are travel communities for young adults, offering unique, curated trips to places around the globe. These are designed to be affordable and hassle-free, with small group sizes and inclusive pricing. Many of the logistics are taken care of for you. One note to mention is that there are often shared accommodations. But hey, you might meet your new BFF. Here are two sample itineraries that sound incredible:

- **To Morocco with the Solo Female Travel Network:** The adventure begins in Marrakech, traverses the Atlas Mountains, and includes camping in the Sahara desert— complete with camels and candlelight. You'll meet local artisans, take cooking classes, and experience a traditional Moroccan spa. The tour finishes with shopping in the bustling city of Marrakech, where you'll find handcrafted goods, textiles, and the scent of spices swirling in the air.
- **To Alaska with Under 30 Experiences:** The trip starts in Anchorage with hiking, wildlife spotting, and glacier exploration. Visit the tallest mountain peak in North America, go on a bear-viewing tour in Lake Clark National Park, and enjoy an authentic Alaskan salmon bake. This expedition is a balance of

adventure and relaxation. Ethically and environmentally responsible, this trip leaves a minimal footprint on the pristine Alaskan landscape.

Potential benefits of guided group tours:

- Doing your first solo trip this way will alleviate a lot of the planning and potential stress of tasks like arranging airport transfers and figuring out transportation while you're there.
- You can take first-hand notes of how things are done to do it yourself on the next trip!
- I'd feel apprehensive about visiting some countries in Asia, Africa, and the Middle East alone. But I would feel much safer with a group and a trusted guide.
- If your parents or loved ones are stressed about the idea of you traveling alone, a group tour could help alleviate their concerns.
- This is a wonderful way to get started if your goal is to make friends with other like-minded travelers.

Sign up for a Workshop or Retreat

Consider booking a trip centered around a workshop

if you're interested in developing a skill or learning something new. For example, if you're a writer or want to pursue it as a hobby, look for writing workshops and retreats. Most are in beautiful locations designed to get your creativity flowing. You'll meet other writers and possibly have a chance to share and workshop your stories.

There are similar retreats for photographers and visual artists. You'll have the opportunity to take photos or create visual art inspired by your surroundings. If you're feeling stuck in your creative life, going some-where new and delving deeper into your hobbies is a refreshing way to infuse excitement into your work.

You could find a yoga retreat where you'll do poses on the beach at sunrise. You can go on a retreat for food-ies, where chefs cook delicious, unique meals for you during your stay. You can go on a ski retreat and enjoy the snow. Whatever your interests, you can find a retreat to let you explore that passion while getting a taste for solo travel.

Some workshops or retreats even include meals and excursions. You might only need to pay for the cost of the workshop plus airfare. All food, drinks, and experiences are often included in the price. Others allow more free-dom, with parts of the day pre-planned, but then you're free to explore the surrounding area and go out for meals alone or with other participants.

Don't know where to start? Peruse a website like

Book Retreats or see if a coach or teacher you already follow is planning any unique retreats.

Volunteer Abroad

OPPORTUNITIES THROUGH INTERNATIONAL VOLUNTEER HQ

Volunteering gives you the chance to visit a new country and make a positive impact while doing so. You'll also have the safety of booking a trip and accommodations through an established volunteer agency and often save money with this type of trip as well.

Organizations like International Volunteer HQ offer flexible options for volunteering abroad. You can choose to volunteer from 1 to 12 weeks, depending on your destination, purpose, and personal schedule. Select your trip according to the type of volunteer work you'd like to do or a destination that sparks your curiosity. The database helps you find positions relating to work such as:

- Animal care and wildlife conservation
- Arts and music
- Childcare and teaching
- Construction and renovation
- Elderly care
- Medical, health, and dentistry
- Women's empowerment

One such volunteer project offered at International Volunteer HQ is a construction and renovation project in Fiji, where you can aid in the repair and improvement of local schools and libraries during the week and visit world-famous beaches on the weekend. Immerse yourself in the Fijian way of life while adding value to the local community. There are dozens of other volunteer opportunities on their website, from sea turtle conservation in Bali to migrant and refugee support in Barcelona.

If your volunteer gig keeps you busy during your entire stay, consider tacking on a few extra days at the end of your trip. Give yourself some time to explore what you didn't have a chance to visit while you were volunteering.

The most important reason to volunteer abroad should be a sincere desire to contribute positively to the lives of others or assist in the improvement of a community. Ask yourself, is this a cause I genuinely care about? Will I be able to utilize or develop skills that I already have?

WORLDWIDE OPPORTUNITIES ON ORGANIC FARMS

WWOOF is an international network that connects volunteers with organic farms. Volunteers (often called "WWOOFers") offer their labor (generally about 4-6 hours a day) in exchange for food, lodging, and the opportunity to learn about organic lifestyles. Learning opportunities could include tasks like poultry farming, vegetable farming, construction, forestry, and taking care of other farm animals. You can gain knowledge on how to grow your own food and understand sustainable farming practices.

WWOOF organizations exist in over 120 countries around the world. I did some WWOOFing on two different farms in England. Lodging ranges significantly depending on where you go. For instance, my first 5-day stay in the Cotswolds was a little rough around the edges. (As in, there was no heater and an outdoor toilet). But I enjoyed my duties there, which included clearing weeds, pruning the garden, and making fresh apple cider. For my second WWOOFing experience in the Yorkshire Dales, I stayed in a beautiful mansion on an estate. I'd recommend thoroughly reading the reviews of the farm you are considering, and be sure there are pictures and a description of where you will be sleeping. WWOOFing was one of the most unique and authentic travel experiences I've had to date.

Let's Recap:

- A staycation is a manageable and cost-effective way to explore your city or neighboring cities.

- While it may initially seem less exciting, venturing out in your own country, potentially by going on a road trip or renting a cabin in the wilderness, is a big step toward becoming a brave solo traveler.
- When you're ready to go abroad, consider destinations where you can communicate in a language you're confident reading and speaking.
- If you're still not sure about going 100% solo, look for group travel tours or volunteer opportunities where many of the logistics will be taken care of.

6

THE PERFECTLY PACKED SUITCASE
LEAVE EXTRA BAGGAGE BEHIND

"Let your memory be your travel bag."
  – Alexander Solzhenitsyn

I'd been driving all day from my previous pitstop on the great American road trip. It's a long drive from Missoula, Montana to Mount Rainier in Washington. It's dark and drizzly when I pull up to my mediocre motel on the outskirts of the national park.

By this point, I know the drill: grab my overnight leopard print bag from the trunk and the green fuzzy blanket I keep on my lap as I drive. It's late, so the motel arranged a self-check-in, and the room is left unlocked with the keys inside on the nightstand.

The room is bland and not ultra-cozy, but I don't mind since it'll be a quick one-night stay, and I know I'll sleep soundly tonight. I forgot something out in the car, so I leave the room and close the door behind me.

Moments later, I return to the motel room door and realize my weary traveler's brain made a dire mistake. It's locked. Immediately I panic. I left the key inside. Oh dear. Oh no.

My first thought is to explain to the front desk the predicament I've gotten myself into. But there is no one there. My cell phone is in the room, so there is no way to call them. I wander the grounds to see if there is anyone who can help me out. It's deserted. At this point, I am on the verge of tears and very much cranky.

My next thought is that I should sleep in my car. Not ideal, especially since I already paid for the room and all my stuff is inside. So I wouldn't say I like that idea.

I wiggle the door knob again. Yep definitely still locked. There are two windows to the left of the door. It looks like I can remove the screen. By some miracle, the window is unlocked. I push it open and awkwardly climb through. Never have I been so happy and relieved to be inside a mediocre motel room.

Planning trip activities is the most fun part of getting ready to travel, but you can't overlook packing. You don't want to leave any necessities behind!

The trick is to balance the need to have everything

with the desire to pack light. Unless you're taking a road trip and can load up your car, you don't want to feel burdened with luggage. It is exhausting and annoying to wear, carry, and pull various bags as you make your way from the airport or train station to your lodgings. (Trust me, I've tried). Traveling light will help you remain comfortable while traveling around a new location.

Travel Light

There is a world where people travel with only a carry-on bag, but that is a world I know nothing about! Try as I might, I can never seem to pack everything in a carry-on. If you can manage it, though, it's amazing because traveling with only the essentials adds a beautiful sense of ease and lightness to your trip. Plus, you won't have to pay fees to check a bag and don't risk the airline losing your luggage. It also speeds up your time in the airport (checking bags and waiting at baggage claim). If you do check a bag, be sure not to pack any important travel items in the rare event that it gets lost in transit. Keep your medications, travel documents, money, and other valuables in your carry-on bag.

Have you ever heard of the 80/20 rule? Also called the Pareto Principle, the 80/20 rule can be applied to many aspects of life. For instance, you may find that 80% of your happiness comes from 20% of your activities, suggesting you should focus more time on those enjoyable activities. In work or school, 80% of your productivity might come from 20% of your most focused time, so honing your ability to prioritize tasks and manage your time effectively is a game-changer. Or you might notice that 20% of your wardrobe accounts for 80% of what you wear, indicating you could simplify your life by decluttering and focusing on quality over quantity.

I bring this up because it directly applies to packing clothes, shoes, makeup, jewelry, and anything else you bring on a trip. Ask yourself what your absolute favorite items are—the things you reach for time and time again. That's the stuff you should pack. Another idea to minimize the number of items you bring is to consider packing in a monochromatic color scheme (such as all black or only neutrals), so you can mix and match without worrying about coordinating outfits.

Sample Packing List

This section covers the necessities I'd suggest packing for any trip. Start by looking up your destination's weather forecast so you can bring the proper attire. Remember that buying certain things, like toiletries, is possible while you're away. For instance, if you're unsure when your period will start on the trip, you can pack a few tampons or pads just in case, and pick some up as needed, depending on your destination. If you're going to a remote location or a cabin in the woods, you'll want to play it safe with essential items like that!

Necessities

- **Important documents:** A copy of your passport, driver's license, itinerary (including addresses), and credit card information. I use Google Docs to create itineraries and have the mobile app downloaded. Toggle the "available offline" button to pull it up even if you're not connected to WiFi. You could print hard copies of your itinerary and other documents to be extra safe. A password manager and digital wallet like Dashlane is a secure way to store important information on your phone.
- **Mini first aid kit:** Bandaids, disinfectant wipes, tweezers, and medicated ointment should do the trick.
- **Medicine:** I prefer bringing headache, stomach ache, and allergy medication from home, as other countries might not have the same brands you know work for you. Also, pack any prescriptions or supplements you take regularly and make sure you have enough for the duration of your trip.

- **Reusable water bottle:** Pack it empty and fill it up after you pass through security at the airport. Collapsible water bottles, like the spiral design from QueBottle.com, allow you to have water on hand wherever you go without an empty bottle taking up precious luggage space. You shouldn't drink the tap water in some places. If that's the case, consider purchasing a personal water filter like LifeStraw.

Clothing

- **Short sleeve and long sleeve basics:** Boody.com sells sustainable clothing made from organic bamboo. Their underwear, activewear, and everyday essentials are ultra-comfortable.
- **Undergarments:** Comfy socks, bras, and underwear are available online at Boody and Negative Underwear. If possible, I like the idea of doing laundry while traveling if needed, so you don't have to pack 16 pairs of socks.
- **Lightweight pants:** Versatile for flights, hiking, or visiting museums. Look for quick-drying and wrinkle-resistant. A pair of black hiking pants or leggings fit in anywhere—it's

nice when items can be dressed up or down. The brand Athletica has comfortable and stylish options. Or check out Indigo Luna for eco-conscious yoga wear.

- **Jeans or denim shorts:** Try to bring just one favorite pair.
- **Dress or jumpsuit:** This is the dream for travel because it's easy to slip on without thinking about which top goes with which bottom.
- **One dressy look:** This will depend on the activities you have planned. If you're going to a national park, you could skip this. But in city destinations, consider options for dinner outings and nightlife.
- **Outerwear:** I'd bring something versatile like a denim jacket and maybe a hoodie if you're in the mood to be cozy.

Footware & Accessories

- **Shoes:** Try to stick to 2-3 pairs. If you have comfortable sneakers that look stylish enough for everything you have planned, that would be ideal. I always bring my workout shoes to hit the hotel gym or jog in the park. You might want to bring something you can dress up as a third pair. I usually go for a pair of black boots—waterproof is best. Wear the most cumbersome shoes on the plane so they don't take up crucial luggage space.

- **Purse or day bag:** Consider a small purse, a fanny pack (thank goodness they're actually in style), or a mini backpack. Crossbody bags are ideal, so they can't be easily grabbed off your shoulder.
- **Sunglasses:** Have to protect those eyeballs.

Extra Considerations for Hot Weather

- **Sunscreen:** A good idea for any place where you'll be out in the sun.
- **Hat or cap:** Sometimes I forget to bring a hat, but I always wish I had one.
- **Swimsuits:** Many hotels and Airbnbs have pool access, so you might want to pack a suit to unwind with a swim. I love Londre swimsuits, which are made primarily from recycled plastic bottles.
- **Insect repellent:** I've found that DEET products work best to fend off mosquitos, but if you want less harsh chemicals, try Sawyer Picaridin Insect Repellent.
- **Wang Prom Thai herbal green balm:** This is a miracle balm for bug bites, sunburn, and minor body aches. It comes in a little jar and

contains a combination of natural ingredients like menthol, eucalyptus oil, and peppermint oil. I would not recommend putting it on your face since it has a very icy effect that can burn your eyes.

- **Sandals:** Fun fact about me is that I kind of hate sandals. Anything in between my toes freaks me out. If you're not a weirdo like me, you should bring some sandals.

- **Bonus tip:** Natural, breathable fabrics like cotton or linen feel so much nicer in a hot climate than something synthetic like polyester.

Extra Considerations for Cold Weather

- **Coat:** Patagonia is not the cheapest option, but I admire their sustainable clothing options and commitment to high-quality items. Check out their fleece collection or a water-resistant winter coat if you expect rain or snow.

- **Gloves, hat, and scarf:** A place like REI has a lot of cozy options to choose from.

- **Bonus tip:** Wool undergarments aren't as itchy as you might expect. These days, performance wool is thin and soft, almost like cotton. It keeps you dry and either warm or cool, depending on your body temperature. It's also anti-microbial, preventing the growth of bacteria and fungus, so it won't smell when you're wearing it or shoving it back in your suitcase.

Toiletries

- **Castile soap:** Multipurpose soap I use as face and body wash. It can also be used to hand wash laundry in the sink (if you run out of clean undies). It's super concentrated, so you don't need to bring a lot, plus it's free of harsh chemicals.
- **Shampoo & conditioner:** Try a solid shampoo & conditioner like the one from Ethique. I like it because it's plastic-free but also less messy than traveling with liquids.
- **Makeup:** This isn't a necessity for everyone, but if you want to wear makeup when you travel, consider buying items that do double duty. For example, a lipstick that you can also use as blush or tinted moisturizer with sunscreen. Ensure each item is under the airline restriction size if you're flying to your destination.
- **Other:** Deodorant, hair care items, a razor, and moisturizer. Small sizes only, since these

items get heavy fast. Keep your toiletries in their own bag or packing cube so it's easy to access and any spilled item won't ruin other items.

Practical Items

You might feel most comfortable when you're prepared for any situation, like having an extra pair of socks when hiking and an umbrella within easy reach. However, when you're traveling, additional items that you don't end up using are cumbersome and take up unnecessary space. I rarely pack an umbrella (though I go back and forth on this one). You can always allocate $100 or so for spur-of-the-moment necessities, like popping into a store and buying an umbrella if you get caught in the rain instead of carrying one around "just in case."

- Depending on your destination, you might need a **travel adapter**. The United States, Canada, and Mexico use Type A and Type B outlets, but electrical outlet types go from A to O, so you want to ensure you can plug in your electronics once you arrive. I'd recommend a universal adapter that works in multiple countries.

- **Portable charger:** These are usually small and sleek, similarly sized to smartphones. My phone always dies on the go—it's nice to have a backup charging bank so you won't feel stranded.
- **Eye mask** and **earplugs** for sleeping.
- **Reusable tote bags for shopping:** Baggu bags are my favorite. They have a ton of cute designs and serve multiple functions—carry it to the beach or use it as a grocery bag or even as a purse.
- **Laptop or tablet:** Feel free to leave this behind and give yourself some screen-free time unless it's needed for work.
- **Notebook** for journaling.

Luggage Options

I use Away luggage because it's sturdy, easy to handle, and spins on 360-degree wheels. I find their medium size suitcase to be the most versatile. (Or try the carry-on!) It's not the cheapest luggage out there, but I splurged because I was tired of everything I bought at TJ Maxx wearing down after a couple of trips. Away has a lifetime warranty on their suitcases that covers any functional damage. Away's luggage and backpack combination is nice because you can wear the backpack or put it on top of the suitcase when navigating through the airport. The backpack can stand on its own, so it's easy to prop between my legs on public transportation. Ultimately quality luggage is a fantastic investment, and you won't regret how much easier it makes your trip.

To organize the items in your suitcase, I love Baggu's 3D zip set. Roll up your clothing and undergarments and put them in cubes to stay organized however you see fit. It helps save time when you're getting ready—you can open your luggage and see exactly what you need to grab.

Let's Recap:

- If you're taking a shorter trip, try bringing a carry-on bag. If you need a bigger bag, join the club. But still, pack the most minimal amount possible.
- The weather will be a significant determining factor in what you need to pack. Weather apps provide forecasts about 10 days ahead, but you can also do a Google search for "weather in Austria in October," for example, to get a general idea of the climate.
- Consider what items you consistently gravitate towards. These are your favorite pieces that should make the cut when packing your suitcase.

7

CONNECTIONS ON THE GO

SHARED EXPERIENCES IN UNEXPECTED PLACES

"What you seek is also seeking you."
– Rumi

I arrive at the train station outside the Yorkshire Dales in northern England. My host greets me as I roll my hefty burgundy suitcase along the uneven pavement. She drives us toward the Markington estate, where I'll be staying for the next nine days. I've signed up for World Wide Opportunities on Organic Farms, which offers homestays in exchange for volunteer work. My duties will include feeding food scraps to the chickens each morning, pruning pear trees, and giving the onsite cabin a fresh coat of hunter-green paint.

The estate grounds are wrapped in the colors of fall —a palette of earthy browns, gray skies, and hints of red in the ivy that climbs the walls. Inside, it's massive. Big enough to get lost in.

The next morning, as usual, it's hard for me to crawl out of bed. The air is damp, and the bed is warm. I layer on my work clothes and head downstairs. The boots I brought are not built for the farm, so I borrow a pair of sturdy black rain boots from my hosts.

The chickens are happy to see me. I dump a bucket of leftover food onto the muddy ground, and they seem to think it's delicious. My next job is over at the cabin. There is nothing I love more than a home improvement project. The wood-paneled exterior needs a little love, so I spend hours painting on a fresh coat in solitude. It's quite meditative.

The British son of the estate owners ventures outside to check on me, bringing me a crisp apple for an afternoon snack. It's a cute gesture.

Days pass, and now it's my last night here. In the evenings, I wind down in the living room by the fire. Harry, the apple fairy, sits on the couch across from me. We get to chatting and discover that we were both born on January 26th. Finding a birthday twin feels unique and special. We lay on the red carpet in front of the fireplace as tall as me. I get the feeling he might be crushing on me, but I'm not particularly skilled at deciphering these sorts of things.

It nears midnight, and I'm ready for sleep. I say good-night and head upstairs to my room. As I lay in bed, my phone dings. It's Harry. His message says:

"Might be a bit forward, but do you want to spend the night with me in the attic?"

I'm a bit taken aback, but I figure this feels like fun. I accept his invitation.

"How do I find you?"

He writes back, "Straight up the stairs. Keep going until you see the light."

Now that you've learned about safety when traveling alone and what necessities to pack, you can focus on one of the most common worries women have when traveling solo—getting lonely!

Apps and Websites

There are plenty of apps and websites you can use to meet people wherever you are traveling to. I don't do a lot of pre-trip connecting, as I prefer to wait until I arrive at my destination. If you want to make connections ahead of time, you can check out Facebook groups geared toward female travelers. Some examples are *Girls Love Travel*, *GoWonder,* and *Solo Female Travelers.*

Social media is another great resource. Look up Instagram location tags or hashtags related to your destination to see profiles of people who have been there or live there. If you do this legwork months or weeks prior to your trip, you have time to get to know people before you're on the road and develop stronger relationships with them.

You can also use apps to make friends, like how the dating app Bumble has a friendship component. Make a profile, share some engaging information about your travels, and see who you meet! You can even use the dating side of Bumble while you travel. Tinder and Bumble are the most universally popular dating apps. If you opt for a paid account on either of these apps, you can change your settings to travel mode instead of just your current location. This way, you can set the location to your destination and do some swiping before you leave for your trip.

Starting Conversations

You might prefer not to use an app, either because you want to stay off screens as much as possible or like to let things unfold as they may. Initiating real-life conversations can be challenging, especially if you're an introvert like me. I like having ideas to help me jump that first hurdle. It's easy to keep to yourself when traveling solo, but these conversation starters streamline the process of talking to locals and other travelers and making friends on the road.

One approach is to focus on questions related to what you'd like to learn about a specific area or destination. Or, if someone catches your eye because of their style, appearance, or demeanor, you can ask questions about them to start a conversation.

Remember these key concepts to initiate a conversation:

- Make a comment about the area
- Ask for help or advice about the location
- Ask a question about their shirt, hat, hair, or something that stands out
- Compliment something about the person

Instead of keeping the conversation surface level and, let's be honest, boring, I think of IRF: Inquire, Relate, and Follow-Up (Sander, 2020). Take one of the conversation starters above and continue the thread.

For example, I might notice someone wearing a band t-shirt. I could comment and say, "I love that band too." They might say, "They're my favorite. I got this when I saw them in concert last year." I could continue the conversation with, "Oh wow, I've never seen them live, but I'd love to. Do you go to a lot of concerts?" I'm giving them more information about myself to establish a connection, then *inquiring* about the concert. When they mention other bands they've seen, I could comment on some of my favorite concerts, which helps me *relate* to the person. Then I could *follow up* by asking about the local concert venues, seeing if they've traveled for shows, or telling them about my city and concert venue. The best thing about IRF is that it never gets old—you can keep using it in the same conversation to keep things moving.

IRF prevents you from shutting down a conversation too quickly. It helps to keep you from asking too many yes or no questions. Open-ended questions encourage the person to think about their answers and give more context and details. For instance, when I ask if they go to a lot of concerts, they could say no and let the conversation end. But if I ask, "How many times have you seen the band?" or "What other bands have you seen live?" then they will give me more information to keep the conversation flowing. If you ask too many yes or no questions in a row, you risk letting the conversation fall flat.

Many introverts worry about saying the wrong thing and often go into silent mode. However, this means the conversation will end, while saying something (even if you worry it's a silly remark) will help the other person get to know you. You establish more genuine connections when you're open and authentic. I find it comforting that the person you're talking to knows nothing about you. Plus, you won't ever see them again if you don't want to. The stakes are low, so be whoever you want to be!

Guided Adventures

If you're not feeling up to navigating apps or approaching total strangers, fear not. There's a fantastic alternative that allows you to socialize and have a blast while doing so: guided tours. You'll embark on a carefully planned adventure that introduces you to new experiences while allowing you to connect with many like-minded travelers.

The best part? You'll all share a common interest and are there for the same reason, whether it's art, history, food, or the sheer awesomeness of the attraction. That common ground makes striking up conversations a whole lot easier. It's an instant icebreaker that paves the way for engaging discussions and memorable connections.

I book 90% of my tours and guided activities through Airbnb Experiences. They are kind of like your personal backstage pass to the local scene. Airbnb Experiences are crafted and led by passionate hosts who know their cities inside out. They're the masters of their craft, the connoisseurs of their culture, and they're here to show you a side of the destination you may not find in a guidebook.

Here are some Airbnb experiences I have thoroughly enjoyed:

- Picking out fresh ingredients at a farmers market in Florence, then cooking an authentic Italian meal with a professional chef
- Snorkeling in the Caribbean Sea among sting rays, tropical fish, and sea turtles
- Sunrise yoga on a bluff overlooking the ocean on Kauai's North Shore
- Silent disco dancing tour through the streets of Liverpool

These experiences aren't your run-of-the-mill group tours. They're intimate, personalized, and often involve small groups, so you can connect with fellow adventurers and form genuine connections. Plus, the hosts are like your local BFFs—they'll share insider tips, tell you the stories behind the sights, and ensure you enjoy your time in their city.

By utilizing apps, social media, and guided experiences, you can connect with other travelers and locals before, during, and after your trip. Whether you choose to venture out on your own or join guided adventures, rest assured that the world is full of opportunities to create meaningful connections while traveling solo.

Let's Recap:

- Look into Airbnb experiences to explore your destination's unique offerings.
- Starting conversations can be daunting, but employing the IRF (Inquire, Relate, Follow-Up) technique and embracing your authenticity will help establish genuine connections.
- Check out a Facebook group where other female travelers hang out.
- Social media and dating apps can connect you to interesting people you may not have otherwise encountered.

8

THE CATCH-ALL CORNER
EVERYTHING ELSE YOU NEED TO KNOW

"I haven't been everywhere, but it's on my list."
– Susan Sontag

The textured painted walls are weathered to perfection. I feel years of history in this room. One slender window lets in filtered gray light, and I relax into the mattress that lies directly on the floor.

I'm sleepy from the long train ride but equally hungry and eager to explore the funky Friedrichshain neighborhood on Berlin's east side. As I walk out into the crisp winter air, I consider my two approaches to exploring a new city. One option is to follow my instincts (should I turn right or left? What looks interesting in that direction?), and the other is to open Google Maps and see what fork & knife icons are close by. In this instance, I decide I'll do some Google Maps scouting to see what's around. Falafel Oase is practically right across the street.

Judging by the pictures, aesthetically, I am not impressed. Typically, I weigh the atmosphere and decor heavily in the perfect dining spot equation. This place I'd describe as more of a "hole in the wall." But the 4.8 stars and single $ sign sway me to try it out.

Between the man's broken English and my non-existent German, I manage to order a spicy falafel wrap. I point to the fillings behind the glass encasement, using my hands so I don't need to figure out the German word for cucumber. I add tzatziki sauce and pepperoncini, and honestly I forget what else was in there. All I know is that it was the best $3 meal I've had on the whole trip. There is little space to stand inside, so I enjoy my meal on the outside stoop. The pita wrap is warm and toasted, with black grill marks on both sides.

I returned to Falafel Oase almost a dozen times before leaving Berlin. And I'd go back again.

Welcome to the catch-all corner, where you will find any bits and pieces of information that didn't find their way into previous chapters. We'll discuss the remaining essentials: passports, visas, staying healthy abroad, what to expect at customs, and navigating cell phone usage. Let's dive into the final practicalities before you set sail.

Passports

If this is your first time traveling internationally, getting a passport should be at the top of your to-do list. In the U.S., routine passport service usually takes 6-8 weeks and 2-3 weeks for expedited service. Apply well in advance of any planned trips! If you already have a passport, know that many countries require it to be valid for at least 6 months beyond your scheduled departure date, so take note of its expiration date.

Visas

Visa requirements for different countries vary depending on your country of origin. The easiest way to find these requirements is through a quick Google search. Some countries, like India and China, require U.S. citizens to obtain a visa before they depart from home. Several countries, like Indonesia and Cambodia, require a visa on arrival, where you will need to present documents and pay a fee to secure a visa once you arrive at customs. And many countries may have visa-free travel where you can stay up to 30, 60, or 90 days.

If you're a United States citizen, the U.S. Department of State provides comprehensive information on the visa requirements for every country. Go to travel.state.gov and search for the country you want to visit. Alternatively, you could use an online tool like VisaHQ to look up information on visa requirements.

Oh, and never overstay a visa!

Practical Tips Upon Arrival in Another Country

- Border officials at customs may ask for proof of onward travel. Roundtrip tickets are an easy way to show onward travel and verify the length of your visit. You will likely be asked further questions if you booked a one-way ticket. If you are not sure of your plans, you can always book a refundable return ticket that allows for schedule changes.
- Immigration officers want to ensure you're not trying to sneak into the country without a plan to leave. They don't want someone unemployed to come looking for work illegally. That is why they may ask about your employment or job back home. Another thing I have heard (but have never been asked this personally) is that they could request to see proof of finances, like a bank statement or pay stub from your employer.
- Have a copy handy of the exact address of where you are staying, such as the first hotel or Airbnb you are checking into. I like to

screenshot the address and have it on my phone so it's easy to access without WiFi.

Vaccinations

The best place to look up the required or recommended vaccines is the World Health Organization (WHO) or the Centers for Disease Control and Prevention (CDC). Yellow Fever is a commonly required vaccine for Central and South American countries and parts of Africa. You can also schedule an appointment to see your doctor and inform them of your travel plans.

Getting Medical Care Abroad

If I have a minor medical concern, I start by finding a pharmacy. There is sometimes a doctor present who can point you in the right direction if there is a medication that will help you. I got a terribly itchy rash on my eyelid once in Germany. A local pharmacy suggested this miracle cream that was gentle enough to use near my eyes, and the rash cleared up in a few days.

I find virtual care a fantastic, convenient solution for non-emergencies. Teladoc Care is an example of virtual healthcare that gives individuals access to medical care remotely. They'll connect you to professionals through secure online video consultations, phone calls, or mobile app messaging. You can seek medical advice, get diagnoses, receive treatment recommendations, and sometimes obtain prescriptions, all from the convenience of your location. Teladoc consultations are currently offered in the United States and Canada. If you're enrolled in the Global Care program, visits with a U.S.-licensed doctor are accessible during international travel.

You could also contact your country's embassy or consulate if you need assistance finding medical care. They can provide recommendations for medical facilities that speak your language. Lastly, if you are staying in a hotel or Airbnb, ask the staff or host for recommendations. They may be able to provide information about nearby clinics or urgent care centers.

Know emergency numbers ahead of time. In many countries, the emergency number is 112 or 911, but looking this up and having it ready on your phone is a good idea.

If you have an iPhone, update your medical ID information under Health Settings. There, you can enter emergency contacts, your blood type, and notes for any medical conditions or allergies.

Capturing Photos & Videos

One of the minor downsides of traveling solo is that you can't easily take pictures of yourself. (Unless you want an endless collection of selfies.) Propping your phone on something and setting a self-timer is usually what I do. Or you can always ask someone to take your picture, which may push you out of your comfort zone, and maybe you'll make a new friend!

Cell phone cameras are impressive these days, and even though I am a photographer, I often use my phone to take pictures. I've also brought a film camera and a couple of rolls of film to document my trip. It doesn't need to be fancy—it could just be an inexpensive point-and-shoot camera from eBay. What I like about film is that you must wait to see the images. With digital cameras, you have an endless number of clicks. But with film, it forces you to slow down and be intentional. Plus, I always look forward to developing the photos when I return home.

I edit pictures taken on my cell phone with the Tezza app. The batch edit feature is the perfect way to boost your travel photos in one fell swoop. In addition to photos, recording short video clips cements meaningful moments in your memory. Maybe you record 30 seconds of people passing by as you sit at an outdoor Parisian café or a quick 10-second clip of waves hitting the shore as you walk on the beach in Bali. I play around with video footage using the 8mm Vintage Camera app from 8mm.mobi. You can share these on social media or keep them for yourself on your camera roll.

Another idea is to hire a local photographer. Flytog-rapher.com connects you with professionals in almost any major city who know your destination well and take stunning portraits in either popular spots or lesser-known locations.

Now, what do you do with all your pretty pictures? It's nice to have digital copies, but I recommend printing your favorites to have a tangible keepsake. After every trip, I order a batch of Artifact Uprising's everyday print sets. I prefer the smaller-sized prints because they feel like the perfect little travel snapshot. On the back of each print, I write the name of the place and the date and store them in a velvet box. I look back at them often.

Cell Phone Usage

If you're traveling out of the country, having a plan for using your phone without spending a fortune on roaming charges is essential. Your options depend on your carrier provider, but I use AT&T's International Day Pass. It's $10 per day and allows me to use my phone as I would at home. You only have to pay if you use your phone's data. So, if you don't use data for a 24-hour period, you won't be charged for that day. If you're connected to WiFi, you can send texts and use apps without needing data. WhatsApp is a popular way to communicate in other countries instead of texting.

A Note on Sustainability

Traveling sustainably is about minimizing negative environmental impacts and supporting local economies. The question is, how can we be more conscious of our impact on the earth and reduce our carbon footprint?

There are a few considerations to keep in mind to lessen the effects of travel on the environment. When possible, opt for train or bus travel over air travel. It's the most fuel-efficient and often offers the chance to see more of the countryside. If you need to fly, choose direct flights to reduce carbon emissions, and consider contributing to a carbon offset program. *Tomorrow's Air* and *One Tree Planted* are great examples of such organizations.

Public transportation, biking, and walking are all sustainable ways to get around when traveling. Consider a hybrid or electric vehicle if driving or renting a car is necessary.

Though I think taking a cruise to see the world sounds amazing in theory, once I started researching, I learned how harsh these giant ships are on the environment; according to a report released by Pacific Standard, a person's average carbon footprint triples while on a cruise, making it worse than flying in terms of emissions per passenger. Many large-scale cruise ships emit an abundance of air and water pollution. Cruises can also lead to over-tourism in port cities, which strains local resources. However, some cruise lines are actively taking steps to reduce their environmental impact by using cleaner fuels, working on marine conservation, and considering how they affect local businesses and communities (Garay, 2023).

When researching places to stay, note if your lodging mentions sustainable practices on their website, such as energy efficiency, recycling, and sourcing local food and goods. You can also support local farmers by cooking or eating at restaurants that source their ingredients locally. If food is being transported from far away, that increases the amount of carbon emissions required to prepare meals.

Lastly, if you visit a state or national park, respect "leave no trace" when hiking or camping. This helps preserve the ecosystem by respecting wildlife and staying on trails. Never remove any rocks, shells, or other natural elements from where you found them. And, of course, be sure to pack up any litter or leftover food properly.

None of us make perfect decisions all the time when it comes to caring for the environment, but it starts with awareness and working toward perhaps being 1% better each day.

Let's Recap:

- Ensure you have a passport valid for at least 6 months after your planned travel dates.
- Not all countries require a visa, but you will need to check that information beforehand.
- When you arrive in a new country and go through customs, you'll need to know the address of where you're staying and when you are leaving the country.
- Accessing virtual medical care is convenient for getting medical advice from afar.
- Contact your cell phone provider to determine what international data plans are available.
- My favorite photo apps and services include Tezza, 8mm, and Flytographer.
- Consider the most environmentally friendly option that makes sense for your trip. Walking, biking, and public or shared transportation (like trains or buses) are among the best choices.

9

OH, THE PLACES YOU'LL GO
INSIDER KNOWLEDGE

"I am not the same, having seen the moon shine on the other side of the world."
– Mary Anne Radmacher

Today is the day I leave Vietnam, after a year of living and teaching here. I wish I could turn invisible and walk these streets with a camera in hand to document what I've seen because words alone cannot explain it. I've observed the people of Hanoi mostly from a distance. With invisibility protection, I would get up close and personal to photograph the men sleeping on their motorbikes on street corners, the women selling sim cards and jackfruit, and the groups of mohawked teenagers hanging by the lake with their short-skirted, high-heeled girlfriends.

When I arrived here, I was told the best way to get

around was by motorbike. The streets of Hanoi are packed with them. For $65 a month, I had my own scooter, a white Yamaha with a bumper sticker left over from the previous renter.

My ride to work was scenic as can be. The back roads meander around the lake, filled with green lily pads and pink flowers during spring. On rainy days, I layered a hooded poncho over every inch of my body and my bookbag with students' graded homework assignments wedged in between my legs. Helmet hair was also a thing.

The time has come to head back to California. Back to the car that I haven't driven in 12 months. Back to traffic laws. Back to loud Americans. Back to family. Back to extra large portions at restaurants and Starbucks on every corner. Back to the United States dollar as I spend my last 20 dong on a Vietnamese iced coffee. Back home.

We've got two types of travelers in this world: the meticulous planners and the spontaneous adventurers. I fall somewhere in the middle. I understand if the thought of doing endless research to map out the perfect itinerary makes you want to run for the hills. You don't have to be a planner if it's not your thing. There's a treasure trove of awesome itineraries online and in guidebooks that other travelers swear by. You can take one of those bad boys, tweak it to fit your needs, and voila! You're good to go.

In this chapter, I've personally gathered a bunch of amazing places based on my globetrotting escapades. We'll cover New York City, New Orleans, Kauai, Bali, and London. All of these places are ones I have visited by myself, and I have hand-selected them with the solo traveler in mind. You'll find suggestions for places to stay, where to eat, what to do, and how to get around. You can follow them to a T, mix and match by adding your interests, or use them as a roadmap to craft your epic journey from scratch.

We'll begin with a quick overview of my favorite resources for planning a trip.

Research Mode: Activated

Books

Hard copies of traditional travel guides like *Frommer's* and *Lonely Planet* are trending out, in my opinion. They feel a bit too generic. Plus, it can be cumbersome to carry around a book everywhere you go. You may prefer to save everything digitally on your phone instead. However, if you are into physical books, the list below features some unique ones that I find inspiring. I always gravitate toward travel guides that don't list every single thing to see and do but rather curate their selections to the best of the best. Here are my picks:

Cereal City Guides (Los Angeles, NYC, Paris, London & Copenhagen)

Quiet London by Siobhan Wall (also available for New York, Amsterdam & Paris)

It's Nice to Be Alone in Paris by Herb Lester (illustrated guides available in tons of cities worldwide)

Wildsam Field Guides (feature USA national parks and road trips)

LUXE Bali (also check out Hanoi, Barcelona & Melbourne)

Online Travel Guides

Here are a few of my favorite online travel guides:

Condé Nast Traveler

Time Out

Solo Female Travel Network

Under 30 Experiences

Where Jess Travels

Curated Hotel Sites

Instead of doing a standard Google search to find hotels, which will give you an overwhelming number of results, I prefer looking at a curated list. Boutique hotels are always my favorite option because they feel more personalized, cozy, and unique than chain hotels. At Design Hotels and Mr. & Mrs. Smith, they've hand-selected beautiful independent hotels. It's free to become a member. After you sign up, you'll have access to exclusive discounts.

DesignHotels.com

MrandMrsSmith.com

Pinterest

I use Pinterest often to find travel guides for a particular city. For instance, I'll search for "boutique hotels in Stockholm" or "best vegetarian restaurants on Kauai," and sure enough, a travel blogger will have a nice little list of her favorites.

My Top Picks: 5 Destinations to Get Started with Solo Travel

Key:
$ = budget
$$ = mid-range
$$$ = splurge
❀ = free activity
☆ = top pick

NEW YORK CITY

Visiting New York City immerses you in dynamic and vibrant cultures. It's known for its iconic landmarks, diversity, and unmatched energy. There is something for everyone: an endless number of museums, shopping options ranging from thrifted to designer clothes, top-notch restaurants from every cuisine in the world, and plenty of free activities like strolling through Central Park.

Why it Works for Solo Travel

New York is a great place for solo travelers because of its walkability. The city's streets are laid out in a straightforward grid pattern. So, unless you're directionally challenged like me, it is a fairly simple city to navigate.

Getting Around

You'll likely arrive at one of three airports: JFK, LaGuardia, or Newark. The easiest option to get from the airport to your hotel is to take a taxi, which will cost between $40 and $70. There are less expensive options utilizing public transportation, like buses and the subway, but I find lugging a suitcase around at the end of a long travel day more trouble than it's worth.

Once you're settled in your hotel and ready to venture out, the city's extensive public transportation system is the best way to get around. The subway initially feels overwhelming, but Google Maps will tell you precisely which routes to take. Hailing a yellow taxi or using Uber or Lyft can be used for shorter distances or when you prefer door-to-door service without extra walking involved.

If you are in the mood to walk, that is a wonderful way to explore, especially in areas with pedestrian traffic, like Manhattan. New York is a city full of walkers!

Driving a rental car can be challenging and stressful due to heavy traffic and limited parking, so I would not recommend going that route.

Practical Tips

- If you plan on taking the subway, purchasing an unlimited weekly metro card for around $33 is cost-efficient.
- Several museums in NYC have free or "pay what you wish" days. For instance, the 9/11 Museum has free admission on Monday evenings from 5:00 to 7:30. The Brooklyn Museum offers free entry on the first Saturday of the month from 5:00 p.m. to 11:00 p.m. There are several others like this! Make sure to check directly on the museum's website in case of changes.
- Spring and fall are glorious times of the year to visit New York. Winter can be brutally cold and snowy, and summer brings a serious dose of heat and humidity.

To Stay

The Ludlow Hotel ◦ *180 Ludlow St, New York, NY 10002* ◦ *$$$* ◦ Located in the vibrant Lower East Side, one of my favorite neighborhoods in New York. The hotel's vibe is loft-like and industrial, with hardwood flooring, handcrafted silk carpets, and Moroccan lamps. It's a 3-minute walk to several subway stations, which makes it an ideal starting point for exploring the city.

The Evelyn ◦ *7 E 27th St, New York, NY 10016* ◦ *$$* ◦ This chic boutique hotel is located in New York City's NoMad district, a block from Madison Square Park. The hotel opened in 1905 and is designed in a historic Art Nouveau style. Nightly rates are considerably lower than other hotels in the area, which is one reason my friend and I decided to stay here on a recent trip to the city.

☆ **Made Hotel** ◦ *44 W 29th St, New York, NY 10001* ◦ *$$* ◦ A hidden gem set in the center of Manhattan. I'd describe the style as modern and warm, with many rooms offering city views. Check out the hotel's rooftop lounge, Good Behavior, and Paper Coffee, a cozy spot to sip an afternoon cappuccino.

The High Line Hotel ◦ *180 10th Ave, New York, NY 10011* ◦ *$$$* ◦ Housed in a red-brick, Gothic-style building that was once part of a seminary, this hotel in Chelsea makes for a unique stay. Each of the rooms is decorated with locally sourced antique furniture. You'll love the detailed woodwork and original stained-glass windows if you appreciate architecture. There is also an Intelligentsia coffee bar and seasonal outdoor bar in the courtyard. The High Line, Chelsea Market, and art galleries are all nearby.

To Eat

Balaboosta ◦ *611 Hudson St, New York, NY 10014* ◦ *$$* ◦ Middle Eastern and Mediterranean fusion. Fresh, locally sourced ingredients featuring dishes like shakshuka, falafel, and za'atar roasted chicken. This comforting dining experience embodies the essence of home cooking with a gourmet touch.

☆ **Roberta's** ◦ *Multiple locations, but check out the one at 261 Moore St, Brooklyn, NY 11206* ◦ *$$* ◦ Laid-back pizza joint in Brooklyn's Bushwick neighborhood. Their wood-fired, artisanal pizzas are ultra delicious. Try their popular Bee Sting pizza, complete with soppressata, honey, and chili.

Time Out Market ◦ *55 Water St, Brooklyn, NY 11201* ◦ *$$* ◦ Packed with variety. I like to wander into a food market if I'm not sure what kind of meal I'm in the mood for. However, I'm always in the mood for healthy yet filling vegan food. BKLYN Wild is located on the 1st floor and offers plant-based comfort food, such as their "unicorn bowl" with purple sweet potatoes, pink lentils, pomegranate, chili coconut yogurt, and mint.

Los Tacos No.1 ◦ *229 W 43rd St, New York, NY 10036* ◦ *$* ◦ Casual pit stop serving Mexican street food at standing tables—simple menu of tacos, tostadas, quesadillas, and aquas frescas.

Oxomoco ◦ *128 Greenpoint Ave, Brooklyn, NY 11222* ◦ *$$$* ◦ Situated in Brooklyn's Greenpoint neighborhood, Oxomoco is a modern take on traditional Mexican cuisine. Grab a table on the patio and try a mezcal cocktail.

Felice on Hudson ◦ *615 Hudson St, New York, NY 10014* ◦ *$$$* ◦ Located in the West Village, Felice on Hudson is an Italian restaurant nestled among brownstones lining charming streets. Inside you'll find warm brick walls and a cozy and intimate dining room. I'm dying over their Pesto Gnocchi made with string beans, crushed burrata, and fresh basil leaves.

Jack's Wife Freda ◦ *Multiple locations, but check out the one in Chelsea at 116 8th Ave, New York, NY 10011* ◦ *$$* ◦ Enjoy comfort food at this casual cafe serving breakfast, lunch, and dinner. There is

something so nice about breakfast served all day.
Why not order waffles at 4:00 in the afternoon?
Next time I go, I am 100% ordering fried zucchini
chips with a garlic-roasted baguette on the side.

☆ **Thai Diner** ◦ *186 Mott St, New York, NY 10012* ◦
$$ ◦ Serves classic Thai food and beverages in a
trendy, kitschy diner-style setting. For an appe-
tizer, try the Roti Kaeng Fak Tong—a turmeric
roti with pumpkin curry. You may want to reserve
a table ahead of time, as it gets very busy during
dinner hours.

To See and Do

There are a few popular attractions you may want to
check out, even if you usually appreciate the less touristy
spots. The extent you immerse yourself in these loca-
tions depends completely on you. Maybe you only want
to pass by for a picture before continuing on to another
location. I skip any tourist destination that doesn't
appeal to me, because there is no need to see something
just because it's famous or well-known. You can save that
time to visit a place you're more interested in instead.

Visit the Statue of Liberty and Ellis Island ◦
Take a ferry out to the island, where you'll find
the Ellis Island Immigration Museum. If you

have relatives who came to the United States through Ellis Island, you can look up their names and learn more about your heritage. Even if you don't have family history relating to this location, it's an iconic attraction with stunning views.

❀ **Spend Time in Central Park** ◦ Have a picnic on the lawn while reading a book or napping in the sun. Or enjoy recreational activities like jogging or biking. Central Park also hosts various cultural events, including concerts and art exhibitions throughout the year.

Chelsea Market ◦ *75 9th Ave, New York, NY 10011* ◦ A fun place to explore if you want to try different treats from food stalls or shop for unique and handmade goods. There's even a Chelsea Market food tour to give you plenty of tastes of the city while teaching you some local history.

Visit a Museum ◦ An array of museums cater to a wide range of interests in NYC. The Metropolitan Museum of Art (the MET), one of the largest and most famous art museums, showcases over 5,000 years of art from every corner of the world. The Museum of Modern Art (MoMA) is home to an impressive collection of contemporary artwork, including works by Picasso, Warhol, and Van

Gogh. For history buffs, the American Museum of Natural History offers a deep dive into the past, from dinosaur fossils to exhibits on space exploration. The Guggenheim, known for its unique architecture and modern art collection, is another must-visit for art lovers. Other notable mentions include the Whitney Museum of American Art, the Tenement Museum, the Brooklyn Museum, the Intrepid Sea, Air and Space Museum, and the National September 11 Memorial and Museum.

❀ **Cross the Brooklyn Bridge** ◦ A fun experience that gives you tons of photo opportunities, both on the bridge and in the neighborhood at the bridge's end. Walk down to the intersection of Washington and Front Streets in DUMBO to capture a classic photo of the bridge.

❀ ☆ **Walk the High Line** ◦ It used to be a railroad track but is now a popular walking trail. There are plants and flowers growing along the sides, so you'll feel like you're strolling through a garden in the sky.

☆ **Peruse the Brooklyn Flea Market** ◦ *80 Pearl St, Brooklyn, NY 11201* ◦ From antique furniture and retro clothing to unique handcrafted jewelry and gourmet food, this market offers a variety of stalls and is a delightful way to spend a weekend discovering local vendors and artisans.

❀ **Wander a University Campus** ◦ NYU's campus near Washington Square Park in Greenwich Village is great for people-watching. You'll see students rushing to class, musicians practicing, artists sketching, and people lounging on the lawn. Near the historic Riverside Church is another stunning campus: Colombia University. Admire the beautiful neoclassical architecture at one of the country's most prestigious colleges.

See a Performance at Company XIV ◦ Going to a show in New York just feels like the right thing to do. Company XIV is a highly acclaimed burlesque performance set in a moody, sultry atmosphere. I'd recommend the Nutcracker Rouge if you are there during the holiday season, but any show they put on is amazing.

☆ **See a show on Broadway** ◦ What's better than getting dressed up and taking yourself to a show? If you're into theatre, dance, art, or music, you can't miss this! You don't need to splurge for expensive seats, either. The theaters are fairly small, so even from the mezzanine level, the experience is amazing. I'd recommend a classic like *Lion King* or *Moulin Rouge*, but new musicals are always being released—like *&Juliet*, which is a comedic, modern take on *Romeo & Juliet* filled with music from the early 2000s.

NEW ORLEANS, LOUISIANA

New Orleans is known for its lively music scene and unique blend of influences from a variety of cultures. You'll find colorful homes with flower beds in the windows, French-inspired architecture with old-world charm, and jazz musicians playing on street corners. If you love listening to music, eating delicious food, and people-watching, this is the place to go.

Why It Works For Solo Travel

With so much energy surrounding you, it's hard to feel lonely. The bustling energy reminds me of New York, though it's slightly dialed down due to its Southern pace. It's easy to explore on foot—its compact layout and pedestrian-friendly streets make it a delight to wander around and fully immerse yourself in the sights and sounds. Walking also gives you a chance to interact with friendly locals, who are known for their hospitality and willingness to share stories and recommendations.

Practical Tips

- New Orleans can get incredibly hot and humid, especially in the summer months. Stay hydrated, apply sunscreen, and dress in light, breathable fabrics. Sudden rain showers are common, so packing an umbrella or a rain jacket would be a good idea.
- Many bars and restaurants in New Orleans offer excellent happy hour deals, usually between 4:00 p.m. and 7:00 p.m.

Getting Around

To get from Louis Armstrong Airport to the French Quarter, I'd suggest either taking the 202 RTA bus or a taxi. It's about a 15-mile journey that could take anywhere from 30 minutes to an hour depending on traffic. The bus ride is just over $1, but also consider that you'll have to then get from the bus station in the French Quarter to your accommodation. Keep in mind that there are limited departure times. Even though the bus is the cheapest option, after a long day of traveling, I prefer curbside service. For that reason, I would opt for a taxi, which shouldn't be more than $40.

Once you arrive in the city center, a popular way to get around is by streetcar. You can download the RTA app to book rides so that you don't need to fumble around for cash. These historic and charming modes of transport are not only functional but also provide a nostalgic experience. The St. Charles streetcar line is particularly famous, taking you through the picturesque Garden District, past grand mansions on oak-lined streets.

If you prefer a more active way of exploring, renting a bike is a lovely way to get around. New Orleans is quite bike-friendly, and pedaling your way through the city allows you to go at your own pace.

As mentioned before, walking is a beautiful way to fully appreciate the unique architecture, lively music, and vibrant culture that make the city so special. If you're not in the mood to walk or need to get somewhere quickly, you could always take an Uber or Lyft.

To Stay

Ace Hotel New Orleans ∘ *600 Carondelet St, New Orleans, LA 70130* ∘ *$$* ∘ An eclectically designed hotel with bohemian charm. The rich color palette makes the lobby extra inviting and cozy.

Take in city views at the rooftop pool by day and check out their on-site live music performances by night. There's an in-house coffee shop and restaurant too, so you can fuel up before leaving the hotel and come back for a low-key dinner.

✰ **Hotel Peter and Paul** ◦ *2317 Burgundy St, New Orleans, LA 70117* ◦ *$$* ◦ This seriously gorgeous historic hotel is a restored 19th-century church and schoolhouse. It blends elegance and charm, and the antique furnishings and decor are different in each guest room for a personalized touch. Concierge services have connections with local experts on a variety of fascinating subjects, including art, architecture, ghosts, history, music, and food—so they can assist with booking tours and activities.

Henry Howard Hotel ◦ *2041 Prytania St, New Orleans, LA 70130* ◦ *$$* ◦ Staying at this hotel in the Garden District feels like you are going back in time. Though it's about a 20-minute streetcar ride away from the French Quarter, you'll be steps from Magazine Street, which is lined with shops and restaurants.

My Curated List of Airbnbs in NOLA ◦ *bit.ly/ airbnb-new-orleans* ◦ My typical requirements for choosing an Airbnb is that it has at least 10 ratings (no new listings) and higher than 4.7 stars. And of course, the aesthetics have to be up to par.

To Eat

Meril ◦ *424 Girod St, New Orleans, LA 70130* ◦ *$$* ◦ Owned by famous chef Emeril Lagasse, so you know the food is top-notch. It's a casual place to grab a bite if you're in the mood for New American plates and a cold glass of local beer.

☆ **Josephine Estelle** ◦ *600 Carondelet St, New Orleans, LA 70130, located inside the Ace Hotel* ◦ *$$$* ◦ The decor fits right in with the overall trendiness of the hotel, so you'll have plenty of beauty to take in while you enjoy your meal. The rigatoni is my favorite, but there's no pasta dish I wouldn't try.

French Market ◦ *1008 N Peters St, New Orleans, LA 70116, located inside the Shops of the Colonnade* ◦ *$* ◦ There are several food vendors and stalls within the market where you can sample traditional New Orleans cuisine and Creole dishes. It's a great place to try local dishes like beignets, gumbo, jambalaya, and po' boys. I'm not a big fan of seafood, but if you are, you should try the infamous cheese shrimp and grits! Grab something to go or sit and appreciate the action around you.

Cafe Du Monde ∘ *800 Decatur St, New Orleans, LA 70116, located inside the Shops of the Colonnade* ∘ *$* ∘ Enjoy your treats in the café, but I chose to get my beignets bagged so I could walk across the street and watch the steamboats traveling on the Mississippi River.

To See and Do

Book a Tour Hosted by a Local ∘ Signing up for a tour will elevate your experience in the city. Try a Street Art and Mural Walk led by an Airbnb host. There are also Garden District tours, Ghost tours, and Voodoo tours, so you are sure to find something to explore your interests.

✿ ✰ **Enjoy Musical Performers** ∘ Jackson Square or Frenchmen Street are great places to hear talented street performers and watch lively parades pass through. The city is teeming with live music venues. There is also a weekly free event at Armstrong Park featuring some of the city's best jazz musicians.

Experience Mardis Gras? ◦ That question mark was intentional. Mardis Gras, the famous festival known for its colorful parades and raucous street parties, happens in February each year. I personally would steer clear, but if it's your vibe, take into account the crowds and inflated pricing.

Go on a Steamboat Cruise ◦ Board an authentic steamboat for a cruise down the Mississippi River. These often come with the option of dinner and live jazz music.

❀ **Appreciate the Architecture** ◦ The Creole houses have a French Colonial style with plentiful, inviting porches and brightly colored exteriors. It's not uncommon to walk from a residential neighborhood decked out with funky houses, to turn the corner and find yourself in front of a stunning cathedral. St. Louis Cathedral is the most famous, built in the 18th century. You might also appreciate St. Patrick's Church and Christ Church Cathedral for equally old, beautiful architecture.

KAUAI, HAWAII

Known as the "Garden Isle," Kauai is a haven of natural beauty and incredible landscapes that will leave you in awe. It's filled with lush rainforests, cascading waterfalls, and pristine beaches fringed by warm turquoise waters. I'd recommend focusing a trip to Hawaii on a single island instead of island-hopping.

Why It Works for Solo Travel

Kauai's relaxed and laid-back atmosphere will instantly put you at ease. It's an ideal getaway if what you need is a place to escape and recharge.

Practical Tips

- Pack for rain. Rain showers happen frequently (especially on the North Shore), so be prepared with a light raincoat or umbrella.
- Plan ahead for popular hikes. Some of Kauai's hiking trails require permits that can sell out months in advance.
- Embrace "Aloha Time." Things move slower in Kauai, and that's part of its charm. Don't rush—embrace the mellow island vibe.

Getting Around

The best way to get around Kauai is by renting a car. After you arrive at the Lihue Airport, follow the signage to pick up your rental car, and you'll have total freedom to drive directly to your hotel or Airbnb.

Public transportation in Kauai is somewhat limited and may not provide access to all the locations you want to visit. A rental car will allow for the most flexibility to explore the island on your own schedule. If you're planning on traversing any rough terrains or plan to visit areas with difficult access, such as Waimea Canyon or Polihale Beach, a 4-wheel drive vehicle could be beneficial. However, for most places, a standard car will suffice.

To Stay

If you haven't figured it out by now, I'm definitely more fond of boutique hotels than large resorts, but Hawaii is one place where big hotels take over. Here is one option: **Grand Hyatt Kauai Resort & Spa** ◦ *1571 Poipu Rd, Koloa, HI 96756* ◦ *$$$* ◦ Upscale accommodations, endless amenities, and a range of dining options.

☆ If you're looking for quietude, I'd highly recommend booking the best Airbnb on the planet: *bit.ly/kauai-airbnb* ◦ This place is really special. It's situated in a somewhat secluded location on Kauai's North Shore and is a short drive to nearby beaches and hiking trails. Every window in the house offers panoramic views of the tropical vegetation and fruit orchards that surround it.

To Eat

Neighbors Café at 1 Hotel Hanalei Bay ◦ *5520 Ka Haku Rd, Princeville, HI 96722* ◦ *$$$* ◦ When a hotel is too expensive for me to stay at, I simply visit their restaurant to experience the atmosphere and get a feel for what it's like to be a high roller. Neighbors Café is a communal spot to grab breakfast, lunch, or an afternoon refreshment like cold-pressed juice. Picture windows offer gorgeous views of Hanalei Bay.

Hanalei Bread Company ◦ *5-5161 Kuhio Hwy #4, Hanalei, HI 96714* ◦ *$$* ◦ A slice of heaven tucked away in the charming town of Hanalei. Enjoy their assortment of organic bread, pastries, and coffee for breakfast. Ingredients are ultra-fresh, as the majority of the food on your plate was picked that morning at their local sister farm Zephyr.

The kitchen closes at noon, but you can still order drinks and smoothies throughout the day.

Nourish Hanalei ⋄ *5225 Hanalei Plantation Rd, Princeville, HI 96722* ⋄ *$* ⋄ A humble food stand crafting sweet and savory bowls, along with specialty drinks and coffee. A healthy spot for a classic açaí bowl or a fresh farmer's market salad.

Trilogy Coffee & Tea Bar ⋄ *4270 Kilauea Rd J, Kilauea, HI 96754* ⋄ *$* ⋄ Opt for a beautifully plated dish or a convenient grab-and-go option to bring with you to the beach. Be sure to try one of their drink concoctions, like Chai tea made with a house-made masala spice blend.

Russell's by Eat Healthy Kauai ⋄ *4-369 Kuhio Hwy, Kapa'a, HI 96746* ⋄ *$$* ⋄ Close to the airport, so it's an easy pitstop on the way to your accommodations. It's a health-centric dining spot serving breakfast bowls, sandwiches, wraps, salads, smoothies, and a selection of vegan and gluten-free dishes.

To See and Do

✿ **Kauapea Beach Trailhead** ⋄ *2868 Kalihiwai Rd,*

Kilauea, HI 96754 ◦ Commonly known as the "Secret" beach, this is a hidden gem. You'll take a short 15-minute walk along a shady path, overhearing surfers talk about the banana pancakes they ate for breakfast, before arriving at one of Kauai's less-busy beaches.

☆ **Hike the Kalalau Trail in Hā'ena State Park** ◦ *6CC9+8R Wainiha, Hawaii, Kapa'a, HI 96746* ◦ An 11-mile hike connects Ke'e Beach and Kalalau Beach. It's a long journey, and I ended up going only about halfway. I almost forgot how tired I was as I admired stunning coastal views of some of the most scenic landscapes in Hawaii. You'll need a reservation to enter the park—I recommend purchasing a shuttle & entry pass ahead of time at gohaena.com.

Waipa Farmer Market ◦ *55785A Kuhio Hwy, Hanalei, HI 96714* ◦ Locals and tourists alike visit this small market on the North Shore on Tuesday afternoons. Get a feel for the island community and support farmers while sampling locally-grown produce like mangoes, papayas, bananas, pineapples, and exotic dragon fruit.

❀ **Tunnels Beach** ◦ Located near Hā'ena State Park, its shallow reefs make it ideal for snorkeling. You may even spot a sea turtle! Swim in the crystal-clear waters with lush green mountains as your backdrop.

☆ **Limahuli Garden & Preserve** ◦ *5-8291 Kuhio Hwy, Hanalei, HI 96714* ◦ Wander these expansive grounds as you admire colorful Hawaiian flora and rare plant species. There are benches dispersed throughout the garden, which offer quiet space to pause for reflection.

Kauai Coffee Farm Tour ◦ *870 Halewili Rd, Kalaheo, HI 96741* ◦ A unique opportunity to visit Kauai Coffee Company, the largest coffee farm in the United States. This plantation produces approximately 60% of all Hawaiian coffee. The tour teaches the stages of coffee production, from the planting of the seed to the brewing of the perfect cup. You can also taste several different kinds of coffee or take a self-guided walking tour through the coffee fields.

Sign up for a Surf Lesson ◦ If you're not afraid of waves, check out the surfing experiences for beginners on Airbnb. On Airbnb's website, toggle from "Stays" to "Experiences" and search Kauai for options on different parts of the island. One local host named Kevin provides a personalized lesson including the basics of surfing—covering everything from paddling techniques to mastering the art of standing up and riding the waves.

✫ **Shop at Hunter Gatherer** ◦ *Suite I-1, 4270 Kilauea Rd, Kilauea, HI 96754* ◦ Brought to you by a passionate seeker of the "coolest sh*t possible," Hunter Gatherer is more than just a store—it's an artistic haven and a goldmine for gift-givers. This curated collection brings together some truly unique finds.

Waimea Canyon State Park ◦ Often referred to as the "Grand Canyon of the Pacific," is one of the must-see natural wonders in Kauai. Cruise along Waimea Canyon Drive, which leads to several lookout points. Choose a hiking trail according to your desired challenge level. The Canyon Trail to Waipo'o Falls is a popular choice, which is about 3 miles there and back.

BALI, INDONESIA

Bali is a province in Indonesia, on the west end of the Lesser Sunda Islands. The following suggestions are for the jungle paradise of Ubud, but if you prefer to stay near the beach I'd recommend checking out Canggu, Uluwatu, or Candidasa. The cultural aspects of Ubud make it a fascinating destination. You can witness unique celebrations and dances and see artisans making and selling their wares. Though it's surrounded by jungles and fields, Ubud is a bustling city with plenty of yoga studios, health-centric restaurants, and boutiques.

Why It Works for Solo Travel

Bali has a welcoming and accommodating culture. It's known for its affordability, which is great for solo travelers who don't want to spend a lot. With affordable accommodations and inexpensive yet delicious local cuisine, your money goes a lot further in Bali.

Practical Tips

- English is the unofficial third language of Indonesia, after Indonesian and Balinese. Most people in Bali speak English, at least at a basic level, so you'll be able to communicate.

This is especially true for the people at your hotel or lodgings, staff at restaurants, and yoga class leaders.

- The area gets a lot of rain between November and March, so planning your trip between April and October is ideal. I have visited during the rainy season, though, so don't let that deter you.
- The bugs are no joke. If mosquitoes like you, don't skimp on the DEET.
- 15,000 rupiahs is equivalent to approximately $1 USD.

Getting Around

Once you land in Bali at Denpasar Airport, you'll need to travel about an hour and a half north to reach Ubud. If you're staying at a hotel, you can contact them ahead of time and ask if they will arrange for a driver to pick you up from the airport. After you exit customs, you'll see lines of drivers holding up signs, just like in the movies. And now you're the star of the movie. Look for your name, and that's your driver, baby! If you're staying at an Airbnb, you can download a transportation app like Grab or Gojek to order a ride to where you need to go.

After you see the layout of Ubud, you might consider renting a motorbike to have more freedom with your transportation. Make sure you drive the motorbike carefully and slowly, understand traffic patterns, and wear a helmet.

To Stay

✰ **Trinity Gardens** ◦ *Jl Subak Sok Wayah, Ubud, Kaja, Gienyar, Bali* ◦ *$$* ◦ A collection of houses surrounded by jungle and rice fields, with mountains as the backdrop. There are six options to book, depending on your space needs, preferred view, and budget. But honestly, it doesn't matter which house you choose because the whole experience at Trinity Gardens is wonderful.

My Airbnb Wishlist ◦ *bit.ly/bali-wishlist* ◦ Stay in your own private villa for prices that don't seem real.

To Eat

✰ **Cafe Pomegranate** ◦ *Jl. Subak Sok Wayah, Ubud, Kecamatan Ubud, Kabupaten Gianyar, Bali 80571* ◦ *$$* ◦ Located in the middle of a rice field, making it one of the most unique restaurants I've ever been to! It's an open-air dining experience with stunning views. You can order all sorts of juices and smoothies to give you energy for your day or kick back at sunset with wine, beer, or homemade sangria. I love sampling several small bites, like dumplings, hummus, and sticky rice.

☆ **Jungle Fish** ∘ *Located in Chapung Se Bali Resort and Spa at Jl. Raya Sebali, Keliki, Kec. Payangan, Kabupaten Gianyar, Bali 80561* ∘ *$$* ∘ Even if you're not staying here, swim and eat all day at this private pool club. Rent a sun lounger or dining table for around $23, plus the cost of food and drinks. Sip on a Jungle Green Juice and fried vegetable spring rolls while you take in the incredible view.

Mother ∘ *Jl. Nyuh Bulan Jl. Nyuh Bojog No.24d, MAS, Kecamatan Ubud, Kabupaten Gianyar, Bali 80571* ∘ *$$* ∘ They serve an excellent breakfast, lunch, and dinner, offering local food that includes gluten-free, dairy-free, nut-free, vegetarian, and plant-based options. Their menu includes salads, soups, sandwiches, or delicious healthy bowls. Choose a tasting plate to experience several different dishes at once.

Alchemy ∘ *Jl. Penestanan Kelod No.75, Sayan, Kecamatan Ubud, Kabupaten Gianyar, Bali 80571* ∘ *$$* ∘ This is the place to visit if you're in Bali to improve your overall health and wellness. Grab a healthy protein bar or acaí bowl at any time of the day. They also make medicinal soups with nutrient-packed ingredients like turmeric, miso, ginger, and bok choi. And last but not least, dessert—try an ice cream sundae or raw sorbet.

Herb Library ◦ *Jl. Jembawan, Ubud, Kecamatan Ubud, Kabupaten Gianyar, Bali 80571* ◦ *$$* ◦ This is a beautiful and relaxing outdoor dining experience. Come for breakfast bowls and sandwiches to kickstart your day and fresh salads and noodles for lunch. Choose from protein bowls, soup, spicy chicken and vegetables, steak, and local fish.

To See and Do

Get Your Yoga On ◦ Ubud is overflowing with yoga studios. It's a relaxing way to start your day or unwind after hours of exploring the area. Check out Alchemy Yoga, Heart Space Bali, or Yoga Barn.

Book a Waterfall Tour ◦ Look at the Airbnb tours and experiences offered in Ubud and book a unique afternoon for yourself. There's a waterfall tour where a local takes you to a hidden location that most tourists never find on their own. You can stand in the waterfall, swim, and take pictures. You can see three waterfalls and learn about the area from a local, which is a great way to get insight into what else to do in Ubud.

Take a Class to Learn a Local Skill ◦ Ubud has plenty of classes for local cultural crafts like traditional Balinese painting, silver jewelry making, and batik dyeing. I found the following classes on Airbnb Experiences, but you could also find a highly-rated service by doing a Google search. The Balinese painting class teaches you how to create a work of art by harnessing the traditional methods of famous artists from Bali. You don't need artistic experience—the teacher helps with inspiration, sketching, and painting. In the jewelry-making class, make your own souvenir while learning a skill. You get about five grams of silver to hammer and carve into a piece of jewelry, either earrings, a ring, or a pendant. Lastly, the batik-making class is a wonderfully unique experience. Batik is a method of dyeing cloth using wax to create a design. You'll get fabric and learn how to apply the hot wax with a stencil before dyeing the fabric. When you remove the wax, an intricate design will be revealed.

✫ **Indulge in a Spa Treatment** ◦ Getting pampered with massages, facials, and body treatments is hands-down my favorite thing to do in Bali. I've been served tea and toast in a tub full of flower petals while overlooking rice fields. If only I could remember the name of that place...A spot I *can* recommend is Karsa Spa. I'm actually dying over the description of their Spicy Balinese Boreh: "*Begin with a 60-minute massage with a warming Ayurvedic oil blend. Next, we exfoliate the skin with a traditional spice blend of cloves, nutmeg, cinnamon, ground rice, and coriander. Finish with a mask of fresh tamarind and Borneo honey, then soak in a hot bath as you sip on ginger and lemongrass tea.*" Yes please, sign me up!

LONDON, UNITED KINGDOM

London is a wonderful destination with fantastic accents that will make you feel like a royal. Appreciate the art, architecture, and trendy fashion in this modern yet historic city.

Why It Works For Solo Travel

London is full of experiences that can be enjoyed alone. You can walk leisurely along the Thames, enjoy a West End show, or sit in a café and people-watch. If you're looking for social events and meet-ups, there are dozens of options that cater to a variety of interests. Plus, there's no language barrier to worry about if you speak English.

Practical Tips

- One thing to remember when planning your London trip is that England is small. If you live in a large country like the United States, you're used to taking hours or days to get from your city to your destination. But England can almost fit in the state of California, so distance and travel times are relatively short. This is especially true when you consider their impressive train system. You can make time to see many different areas of the country while keeping London as your home base.

Getting Around

There are a lot of airports in London, but I'll explain how to get from Heathrow Airport to the city center, since that is one of the more popular airports. It's a good idea to check Google Maps to see which routes are suggested to get you to your accommodation. Change the "depart" time because the best options and routes may change depending on the time of day. I always like to arrive at a new travel destination during the day (and never late at night) because I find it easier to navigate the world before it gets dark. Spoken like an actual grandma. If Google Maps suggests a route requiring multiple transfers from one subway line to another, or if more than 0.5 miles of walking is needed, I think taking a taxi or Uber is worth it. It may cost up to $100, but when you've had a long day of traveling and are carrying all your bags, the price tag is worth the convenience.

The easiest and most popular way to get around in London is by using the city's public transport system, which includes the London Underground (also known as the Tube), buses, trams, overground trains, and river buses. The Tube has 272 stations in the city and is particularly convenient for quick travel. The red double-decker buses are slower than the Underground but are great for short distances or if you want to take the scenic route. Public transportation is very user-friendly and can get you anywhere you want to go in the city and beyond. Again, Google Maps will be your best friend.

If you have a contactless way to pay on your phone, such as Apple Pay or Google Pay, you don't need an Oyster Card (which cost £7). You'll simply hold your phone up to the card reader to pay for each ride. If you purchase an Oyster card from one of the machines, you'll need to load money onto it throughout your trip.

If you're more active and the weather is cooperating, you could ride a bike using Santander Cycles, London's self-service bike-sharing system. Prices begin at £2. This would be a nice option for riding around a park or other open space, but perhaps not so much in a crowded part of town (Love and London, 2022).

Finally, walking is a delightful way to explore, especially within a particular area or neighborhood. It's worth noting that London is a large city, so walking from one end to the other might not be practical, but strolling around places like the South Bank, Covent Garden, or Soho is absolutely lovely.

To Stay

Artist Residence London ◦ *52 Cambridge St, Pimlico, London SW1V 4JD* ◦ *$$* ◦ The charming townhouse has 10 rooms with trendy decor and fantastic art on the walls. The bar and café in the lobby offer delicious food for breakfast, brunch, lunch, and dinner. It's a cozy environment that gives you a chance to talk to other guests from the hotel, as well as people in the neighborhood stopping in for a drink or meal.

The Buxton ◦ *42 Osborn St, London E1 6TD* ◦ *$* ◦ Experience Brick Lane's unique bistro and hotel. With just 15 cozy bedrooms, you can enjoy a comfortable stay in the heart of this vibrant neighborhood. Hotel guests can also take advantage of the rooftop area, where they cultivate fresh herbs used in the kitchen and bar. On the ground floor, you'll find a lively cocktail bar and pub, as well as a restaurant offering delicious dining options. Whether you're seeking a relaxing retreat or a lively night out, this hotel has something for everyone.

The Culpeper ◦ *40 Commercial St, London E1 6TB* ◦ *$* ◦ Located in the heart of London, this cozy retreat on the corner has a ground-floor pub, a first-floor restaurant, bedrooms on the second floor, and a rooftop garden.

Mama Shelter London ◦ *437 Hackney Rd, London E2 8PP* ◦ *$* ◦ Channeling her coolest vibes, Mama has created a homey retreat in the heart of

London's trendy East End. Complete with an eccentrically decorated restaurant, an enchanting garden bar, and groovy Japanese-inspired karaoke rooms, Mama gives you the ease of exploration with a dash of fun. Conveniently located near the Bethnal Green underground station and just a skip away from Shoreditch.

Remember, even if you don't book a night in these hotels, you can stop by to enjoy an afternoon cappuccino or glass of red wine in the lobby.

To Eat

The Locals Café ◦ *8 Gatliff Rd, London SW1W 8DT* ◦ *$$* ◦ Located in Chelsea, they offer healthy food options with fresh produce and natural ingredients. The restaurant also follows environmentally friendly practices in composting and disposing of waste, so I feel great about supporting their mission. Their breakfast and brunch menu includes pumpkin pancakes, lobster Benedict, and Turkish eggs. Lunch and dinner options include delicious sandwiches, burgers, and stir-fries. Sip on lattes, lemonade, tea, or wine.

BOXPARK ◦ *2-10 Bethnal Grn Rd, London E1 6GY* ◦

$ ◦ Several food options in one place. You can eat Argentinian, Greek, Singaporean, Spanish, and vegan food. There are also bars with beer, wine, and cocktails to wind down at the end of the day.

Dishoom Shoreditch ◦ *7 Boundary St, London E2 7JE* ◦ *$$* ◦ A bustling Indian restaurant in London's trendy Shoreditch district. It pays homage to the Irani cafés and the rich history of Bombay. The décor, which includes vintage Bombay photos and historical pieces, exudes nostalgia. The menu features everything from traditional biryanis and curries to signature Bombay comfort foods and all-day breakfasts.

Curled Leaf ◦ *98 Mill Ln, London NW6 1NF* ◦ *$$* ◦ Tucked away in a quieter part of the city in West Hamstead, everything is homemade. You get a sense of being in your mother's kitchen, with its open layout and warm wooden communal dining table. You can feel the love put into each and every dish.

To See and Do

❀ ☆ **Tate Modern Museum** ◦ *Bankside, London SE1 9TG* ◦ One of my favorite museums is Tate

Modern, an art museum that covers over one hundred years of design styles. The museum has free entry, so it's worth visiting to see iconic works from Andy Warhol, Salvador Dali, Pablo Picasso, Wassily Kandinsky, and more.

British Museum ◦ *Great Russell St, London WC1B 3DG* ◦ Track human culture from its inception to now with exhibits including history, art, and culture. The museum's permanent collection is one of the largest in the world, so the information you see here is more comprehensive than similar museums. There are exhibits on hieroglyphics, paper-making and books, art history, the Era of Reclamation, the Bronze Age, and more. You don't have to worry about making time for this museum on your busy days because it's open late on Fridays, so you have more opportunities to stop in.

☆ **Brick Lane Vintage Market** ◦ *85 Brick Ln, London E1 6QL* ◦ A supremely cool place if you like to shop or want to find unique souvenirs for your friends and family. There are rows of vintage fashion, ready for you to shift through it all. There are also records, retro accessories, and art. Keep in mind you have to fit whatever you buy into your luggage to fly home unless you decide to ship it separately. Sometimes that thought is the only thing that keeps me from blowing my entire budget at Brick Lane Vintage Market!

❀ **Columbia Road Flower Market** ◦ *Columbia Rd, London E2 7RG* ◦ A fragrant and colorful Sunday market transforms Columbia Road into a botanical paradise. The market offers domestic and exotic plants and flowers, from towering banana trees and delicate orchids to rustic bouquets of seasonal blooms. Victorian shops line the streets, selling vintage goods and baked treats. I was so overwhelmed by the charm of it all that I actually started tearing up walking down the street. Anyway! The whole day is a wonderful experience filled with delightful sights, scents, and sounds.

❀ ☆ **Hampstead Heath** ◦ Be sure to visit this park in north London. Its expansive meadows and towering trees cover over 800 acres. This park is the setting that inspired C.S. Lewis to write *The Chronicles of Narnia*, so you're going to feel some magic as you take in the natural beauty. I love to read or write in my journal. You could also pack a picnic and enjoy the views, which are some of the best in London. There are pubs and restaurants nearby, so you can grab something to take to the park or stop in before or after your relaxing visit.

❀ **Hyde Park** ◦ One of London's eight royal parks, is a beautiful spot if you want to get away from the city's high energy. You can swim in the Serpentine Lido, an open water location that's open from May to September. Hyde Park also has facilities for horseback riding and tennis, if you're looking for a fun way to get your exercise in.

❀ **Green Park** ◦ Another Royal Park right near Buckingham Palace. The vivid grass meadow has fountains and statues in memory of many well-known British citizens, so you can learn some history while enjoying the outdoors. One histor-ical tidbit I learned is that King Charles II's wife forbade all flowers from the park after she caught her husband picking blooms to give to another woman. Though that story is from the 17th century, there are still no flowerbeds in the park. However, if you visit in spring, you'll see wild yellow daffodils in bloom.

Bath ◦ While you can easily find plenty to do in London, you could take day trips to explore nearby areas in the countryside. On one visit, I dedicated a day to travel to a small town called

Bath, which has Roman ruins and stunning architecture. The river that runs through the city inspired me to stop at a restaurant called the Pump Room. Here you can drink a glass of hot spa water that's come straight out of the Earth! The water contains natural minerals that are supposed to be super good for you. It didn't taste great, but it was a unique experience, and I'm glad I did it in the quest for eternal youth!

Let's Recap:

- If you're feeling overwhelmed about where to take your first solo trip, start with one of these five suggestions—New York City, New Orleans, Kauai, London, or Bali. Begin by booking your flight or accommodations, then let the rest fall into place.
- If these suggested destinations aren't calling your name, peruse some online travel guides like Condé Nast Traveler or Design Hotels until you find what speaks to you. Just be careful not to get stuck in research mode forever. Pick a spot and go for it!
- Consider the easiest ways to get around in the place you're visiting. Plan how to get from the airport to your lodging. Have a general idea of

what to expect, and once you get there, you can adjust to what feels best for you.

- After you decide on your destination, save your favorite restaurants, coffee shops, stores, museums, and other attractions on Google Maps. That way, you'll have the addresses saved on your phone wherever you go.

CONCLUSION

So, does solo travel still sound so intimidating? I hope this book has inspired you to travel on your own, whatever that looks like for you. Maybe it's a staycation, a weekend getaway, a trip to another state, or a volunteer opportunity abroad. You'll feel prepared and safe after researching your destination, trusting that your intuition will guide you in the right direction. You'll know exactly what to pack without bringing your entire life with you on the road. You'll craft the perfect itinerary with a combination of popular destinations and offbeat attractions while still allowing time for the spontaneity of the unexpected. You'll make meaningful connections with locals and fellow travelers or enjoy the peacefulness that solitude brings.

I'd like to leave you with a travel manifesto. A manifesto is a meaningful reminder of the principles you wish to uphold as you explore the world. It includes core beliefs, values, intentions, and aspirations. What is driving you to travel? You can use the following words or perhaps get inspired to create your own manifesto. This is a powerful way to clarify your thoughts and spark action.

My Traveler's Manifesto:
Explore the World with Bravery and Passion

I will approach every destination with an open heart and an open mind. I will seek to understand and appreciate the diverse cultures, traditions, and people I encounter. I will celebrate our similarities as well as our differences.

I will step out of my comfort zone and embrace uncertainty. I recognize that some of the most rewarding experiences come from the unfamiliar.

I will be grateful for the opportunity to travel and for the wonder of the world.

I will use my experiences to inspire and educate others, sharing the beauty and importance of travel.

I will make an effort to connect with others in the community. I will support local businesses to contribute to the places I visit.

I will be a responsible traveler, taking care to protect the environment. I will minimize my impact on natural habitats, respect wildlife, and support eco-friendly practices whenever possible.

I will not rush through my itinerary but instead savor each moment. I will prioritize quality over quantity, allowing time for relaxation and reflection.

I will approach each journey as an opportunity for personal growth and education. I will seek to expand my horizons and learn new skills.

I will remain open to the magic of travel, allowing each journey to inspire awe, curiosity, and a deeper connection to the world and its inhabitants.

SPREAD THE TRAVEL BUG

One trip is all it takes to catch the travel bug, and once you've taken it, you'll be looking ahead to your next opportunity. This is your chance to spread the excitement!

Simply by sharing your honest opinion of this book and a little about your own plans (or trips you've already taken), you'll show new readers how they can get started on an empowering journey of their own.

Thank you so much for your support. Happy traveling! **To leave a review on Amazon, scan the QR code below:**

FREE BONUS: RESOURCES & LINKS

Want every link mentioned in this book, all in one place? I've created a PDF bonus guide where you'll find click-able links for each resource, product, Airbnb wishlist, and website you need to fully prepare you for your next journey.

Go to <ins>bit.ly/solo-travel-resources</ins> or scan the QR code below to download:

77 REASONS YOU SHOULD
TRAVEL SOLO

1. To inspire friends and family to be brave and do the same.

2. To romanticize your life.

3. Because you've been dreaming about it forever, and "someday" is not a day of the week.

4. To live life to the fullest.

5. Prove to yourself that it's possible.

6. Practice self-sufficiency.

7. Restore your faith in humanity.

8. Stop waiting around for others and take matters into your own hands.

9. Because you are worthy of living the life you imagine for yourself.

10. So you can tell your kids and grandkids all your travel stories one day.

11. Foster self-discovery and self-awareness.

12. Develop independence and self-reliance.

13. Complete freedom to choose your itinerary and change plans on a whim.

14. Embrace spontaneity.

15. Marvel at the kindness of strangers.

16. Develop a greater sense of empathy.

17. Seek excitement and novelty.

18. Cultivate a spirit of lifelong learning.

19. Find the confidence to strike up conversations with strangers.

20. Prioritize experiences over possessions.

21. Develop the courage to take risks and seize opportunities.

22. Learn to trust your instincts.

23. Build confidence in decision-making.

24. Meet new people from diverse backgrounds.

25. Deepen cultural understanding.

26. Gain a fresh perspective on life.

27. Discover your limits and push past them.

28. Uncover hidden gems off the beaten path.

29. Learn to be comfortable with your own company.

30. Develop problem-solving skills.

31. Strengthen adaptability.

32. Enhance communication skills.

33. Learn local phrases in a new language.

34. Discover your true interests and passions.

35. Find inner peace and solitude.

36. Reflect on life and future goals.

37. Exercise budget and finance management skills.

38. Gain a sense of accomplishment.

39. Boost creativity and inspiration.

40. Enhance photography and storytelling skills.

41. Try new foods and flavors.

42. Step away from routines and break free from daily monotony.

43. Cultivate camaraderie by bonding with fellow travelers and sharing stories.

44. Face unknown situations with bravery.

45. Develop research and planning skills.

46. Learn about geography firsthand.

47. Recharge and de-stress.

48. Reconnect with nature.

49. Embrace minimalism as you pack only the essentials.

50. Overcome language barriers.

51. Practice mindfulness and meditation in serene places.

52. Celebrate the freedom of the open road.

53. Conquer fears and phobias.

54. Discover your strengths and weaknesses.

55. Appreciate your home country and everyday life.

56. Challenge stereotypes and prejudices.

57. Volunteer and give back to communities.

58. Build resilience.

59. Experience various modes of transportation.

60. Explore local art and culture.

61. Attend festivals and events.

62. Immerse in historical sites and museums.

63. Visit UNESCO World Heritage Sites, national parks, and other natural wonders.

64. Go off-grid and disconnect from technology.

65. Experience the magic of solo sunsets.

66. Marvel at the night sky in remote areas.

67. Discover your travel style by gaining a deeper understanding of your own preferences.

68. Learn to read maps, navigate, and improve your sense of direction.

69. Encounter wildlife in their natural habitats.

70. Experience different climates and seasons.

71. Gain environmental awareness.

72. Explore the world's diverse religions.

73. Embrace the joy of solitude.

74. Build a lifelong sense of adventure.

75. Reflect on the impermanence of life.

76. Cultivate gratitude for your experiences.

77. Because why not?

REFERENCES

Arikoglu, L., & Carey, M. (2021, July 28). *Answering Your Questions About Passport Renewal, Solo Travel, and More: Women Who Travel Podcast.* Condé Nast Traveller. https://www.cntraveler.com/story/answering-your-questions-about-passport-renewal-solo-travel-and-more-women-who-travel-podcast

Countries and Areas List - United States Department of State. (n.d.). United States Department of State. Retrieved August 7, 2023, from https://state.gov/countries-and-areas-list

Fielding, S. (2019, August 8). *New Study Shows 91 Percent of Fears Don't Come True. Best Life.* https://bestlifeonline.com/anxiety-vs-reality-study

Garay, E. (2023, February 27). *Sustainable Ships: The World's Most Eco-Conscious Cruises.* CNN. https://www.cnn.com/travel/article/eco-conscious-sustainable-cruises-cmd/index.html

Horowitz, J. (2017, July 31). *Tips on Tipping Abroad: A Global Gratuity Guide.* Blog | Western Union. https://www.westernunion.com/blog/en/global-tipping-guide

How to Get from Louis Armstrong Airport (MSY) to New Orleans' French Quarter. (2021, December 14). YouTube. https://www.youtube.com/watch?v=3IIS2BLZngc

James, S. (2023, March 2). *The Cheapest Nicest Hotels in London.* Condé Nast Traveller. https://www.cntraveller.com/gallery/best-cheap-hotels-london

Life360 | Family Tracking App | Location Sharing & Family Safety. (n.d.). Life360. https://www.life360.com

Lightning Bug Electric. (2021, April 9). *Why Do Different Countries Use Different Plugs?* Marietta Electrician. https://www.lightningbugelectric.com/blog/2021/april/what-plugs-are-used-in-different-countries

Love and London. (2022, June 30). *What to know about every public transport in London - Train vs boat vs bike vs cable Car.* YouTube. Retrieved

August 25, 2023, from https://www.youtube.com/watch?v=raF0-wkJrqU

Marrazzo, L. (2022, February 14). *Most Popular Dating Apps per Country*. AppTweak. https:///mobile-app-news/check-out-the-most-popular-dating-apps-by-country

OpenAI. (2023). *ChatGPT* (Version 3.5) [Large language model]. https://chat.openai.com/chat

Rich, K. (2023, February 16). *What to Pack for a Trip to a Conservative Country*. The Blonde Abroad. https://www.theblondeabroad.-com/what-to-pack-for-a-trip-to-a-conservative-country

Sander, V. (2020, October 22). *How to Make Conversation as an Introvert*. SocialSelf. https://socialself.com/blog/make-conversation-introvert

Travel Advice and Advisories. (n.d.). Travel.gc.ca. https://travel.gc.ca/travelling/advisories

Whitman, B. (2009, June 22). *The Essential Guide for Women Traveling Solo*. Dispatch Travels.

Wolff, D. G. (2003). *The Girl's Guide to Traveling Solo*. Trafford Publishing.

Women Peace and Security Index. (2021). In *Georgetown Institute for Women, Peace and Security*. Retrieved August 8, 2023, from https://giwps.georgetown.edu/wp-content/uploads/2021/10/WPS-Index-2021-Summary.pdf

Made in the USA
Las Vegas, NV
25 November 2023

81491733R00111